Mastering Multi-Agent Systems in Python: AI, Automation, and Coordination

Ryan C. Lofton

Preface

We live in a world where **intelligent agents** surround us. From **autonomous drones coordinating deliveries** to **AI-driven trading systems optimizing financial decisions**, the influence of **multi-agent systems (MAS)** is expanding across industries. These systems go beyond individual AI models by enabling **multiple agents to work together, learn, and adapt**—just like humans in a team.

Despite their growing importance, multi-agent systems remain a **complex and often misunderstood** area of artificial intelligence. Many developers and researchers hesitate to explore MAS due to its perceived difficulty, especially when it involves **game theory, reinforcement learning, or large-scale distributed systems**. This book aims to **bridge that gap** by making MAS approachable, practical, and actionable.

Why This Book?

The goal of this book is **not just to explain MAS concepts but to guide you in building them**. Theory is essential, but real understanding comes from **hands-on implementation**. Whether you're a developer, researcher, or AI enthusiast, this book provides a **structured, step-by-step approach** to designing, developing, and optimizing multi-agent systems.

Here's what makes this book unique:

- **Practical, Code-Driven Approach** – Each concept is reinforced with **fully functional Python examples**, ensuring you can apply what you learn.
- **Real-World Applications** – We go beyond abstract theory to explore **how MAS power robotics, traffic systems, finance, and even smart cities**.
- **Scalability and Optimization** – We discuss **testing, debugging, and deploying** MAS at scale, ensuring your systems are **efficient and reliable**.
- **Ethical and Security Considerations** – As MAS become more autonomous, ensuring **fairness, security, and transparency** is critical. We explore the challenges and solutions in depth.

Who Should Read This Book?

This book is designed for:

- **AI and ML Engineers** wanting to integrate multi-agent systems into their projects.
- **Developers** looking to explore coordination, automation, and AI-driven decision-making.
- **Researchers** interested in reinforcement learning, game theory, and evolutionary strategies for MAS.
- **Anyone curious about how intelligent systems can work together** to solve complex problems.

Whether you're a beginner in MAS or an experienced AI engineer, this book will provide **a clear roadmap to designing and implementing MAS effectively**.

How This Book is Structured

The book is organized into **ten chapters**, each covering a critical aspect of MAS development:

- **Chapter 1-3** introduce **the fundamentals**, covering MAS architectures, types of agents, and communication strategies.
- **Chapter 4-6** dive into **designing, training, and optimizing** MAS, exploring rule-based, learning-based, and evolutionary approaches.
- **Chapter 7** explores **real-world applications**, showing how MAS are used in robotics, finance, healthcare, and beyond.
- **Chapter 8-9** focus on **testing, debugging, and deploying MAS at scale**, ensuring they perform efficiently.
- **Chapter 10** discusses **future trends, ethical concerns, and the next steps for MAS development**.

Each chapter combines **conceptual explanations, practical coding tutorials, and real-world insights** to provide a well-rounded learning experience.

Final Thoughts

The field of MAS is evolving rapidly, offering **new opportunities for innovation in AI, automation, and distributed intelligence**. By the end of this book, you'll not only understand the core principles of MAS but also be equipped with the skills to **build and deploy your own multi-agent systems**.

Let's dive in and explore the exciting world of **intelligent agents working together to solve real-world problems**.

Table of Contents

Chapter 1: Introduction to Multi-Agent Systems

Multi-Agent Systems (MAS) are at the core of many intelligent systems, from robotics swarms to AI-driven simulations and financial trading bots. If you've ever wondered how self-driving cars coordinate at intersections without chaos, how AI-powered game characters collaborate, or how decentralized systems manage complex tasks, you're already thinking in terms of MAS.

This chapter will introduce you to the fundamental concepts of Multi-Agent Systems, why Python is an excellent language for developing them, and some exciting real-world applications. By the end, you'll have a strong foundational understanding and be ready to start building your own intelligent agents.

1.1 What Are Multi-Agent Systems (MAS)?

Imagine a busy beehive. Each bee has a specific role—some gather nectar, others protect the hive, and a few manage internal tasks. No single bee is in charge, yet the colony thrives through coordination, communication, and self-organization. This is a natural example of a **multi-agent system (MAS)** in action.

A **multi-agent system** is a system composed of multiple autonomous entities, known as **agents**, that interact with each other and their environment to achieve individual or collective goals. These agents can be physical entities like robots or purely digital ones like AI models in simulations. They operate based on predefined rules, learned behaviors, or adaptive decision-making processes.

Breaking Down the Concept

To understand MAS better, it's helpful to think of it as an extension of traditional AI. Instead of a single intelligent system handling all decision-making, MAS distributes intelligence among multiple interacting agents. This approach offers advantages such as decentralization, scalability, and robustness.

Each agent in an MAS can:

- **Sense its environment** and react accordingly.
- **Make decisions autonomously** based on predefined rules or learning algorithms.
- **Communicate with other agents** to share information or collaborate.
- **Adapt its behavior** based on past experiences or external changes.

Unlike centralized AI models, where a single system makes all decisions, MAS distributes intelligence across multiple entities, allowing for more flexible and resilient problem-solving.

How MAS Differs from Traditional AI

Traditional AI often focuses on optimizing a single intelligent system—like a chess-playing AI that calculates the best move for one player. In contrast, MAS involves multiple entities working together, sometimes cooperatively and other times competitively. This difference makes MAS especially valuable in **complex, dynamic environments** where no single system has complete control or perfect information.

For example, in **robotic swarms**, multiple robots must coordinate their movements without a central controller. If one robot encounters an obstacle, the others must adjust their actions dynamically. This decentralized approach mimics natural systems like flocks of birds or schools of fish, where local interactions lead to emergent, large-scale behavior.

The Power of Interaction

What makes MAS unique is how agents interact. These interactions can take many forms:

- **Cooperation:** Agents work together to achieve a shared goal. Think of warehouse robots collaborating to transport packages efficiently.
- **Competition:** Agents have conflicting objectives, such as AI traders in financial markets competing for profit.
- **Negotiation:** Agents communicate to reach mutually beneficial agreements, often seen in automated contract bidding or supply chain management.

The ability of agents to **learn from each other** and **adapt to their environment** is what gives MAS its strength. A well-designed MAS can handle uncertainty, distribute workloads efficiently, and scale naturally as more agents are introduced.

Real-World Inspiration

Many MAS applications are inspired by biological and social systems. Just as ants work collectively to find food without a central leader, MAS can be used in logistics to optimize delivery routes. Just as human societies rely on negotiation and resource-sharing, MAS can model and improve real-world economic systems.

MAS is more than just a theoretical concept; it's the foundation of many modern AI applications. Whether in robotics, gaming, smart cities, or decentralized AI networks, MAS enables **intelligent, adaptive, and scalable** problem-solving.

In the next sections, we'll explore why Python is a great language for building MAS and examine its most impactful real-world applications.

1.2 Why Use Python for MAS?

Multi-Agent Systems (MAS) can be complex, requiring sophisticated coordination, communication, and decision-making strategies. Choosing the right programming language is crucial to ensure flexibility, ease of development, and integration with modern AI tools. **Python** has emerged as the language of choice for MAS development, offering a powerful combination of simplicity, versatility, and an extensive ecosystem of libraries.

The Role of Python in Multi-Agent Systems

Python's dominance in AI and automation makes it a natural fit for MAS. It simplifies the development of agents by providing high-level abstractions while still allowing deep customization when needed. Unlike lower-level languages such as C++ or Java, which offer performance benefits but require more complex syntax, Python allows developers to focus on designing intelligent behaviors without being bogged down by implementation details.

In MAS, agents often need to communicate, learn, and adapt. Python provides built-in tools for handling these tasks efficiently. Whether an agent is making autonomous decisions using **machine learning**, coordinating with others via **message passing**, or simulating complex interactions in a **virtual environment**, Python has specialized libraries to handle each aspect.

Why Python Stands Out for MAS Development

One of Python's greatest strengths is its ability to **accelerate prototyping**. MAS development often involves experimentation—tweaking agent behaviors, testing new communication protocols, and optimizing interactions. Python's dynamic nature and ease of use make this process seamless, allowing developers to iterate quickly and refine their models.

Another major advantage is Python's **extensive library support**. Libraries like **Mesa** simplify agent-based modeling, **SPADE** enables communication between distributed agents, and **Gym** provides reinforcement learning environments for training intelligent agents. Instead of building everything from scratch, developers can leverage these tools to focus on higher-level system design.

MAS also requires **scalability**. While Python isn't the fastest language, it integrates well with high-performance computing tools such as **NumPy**, **Cython**, and **Ray**, allowing developers to run large-scale multi-agent simulations efficiently. Cloud computing platforms and parallel processing frameworks further extend Python's capabilities, making it possible to deploy MAS solutions in real-world applications.

Bridging MAS with AI and Machine Learning

Python is the primary language for AI research and development, and MAS often intersects with machine learning. Many MAS applications involve **adaptive agents** that learn from their environment using **reinforcement learning**, a field dominated by Python-based frameworks such as **TensorFlow**, **PyTorch**, and **Stable-Baselines3**. These tools enable agents to evolve their strategies over time, improving their decision-making in dynamic environments.

In competitive MAS settings, such as **AI-driven trading systems** or **game AI**, agents must analyze patterns and adjust their behavior accordingly. Python's AI ecosystem provides a rich set of tools to implement and fine-tune such adaptive strategies.

The Flexibility of Python for Different MAS Architectures

MAS can take various forms, from **fully decentralized** systems where each agent operates independently to **hierarchical** structures where a central entity coordinates tasks. Python's flexibility allows developers to implement these architectures with ease.

For decentralized systems, Python supports **peer-to-peer networking**, **asynchronous communication**, and **message passing**, which are critical for real-time agent interactions. For hierarchical MAS, Python's object-oriented design and modularity make it easy to manage complex agent structures and behaviors.

A Language Backed by a Strong Community

One of Python's greatest assets is its community. The language has a vast number of developers, researchers, and open-source contributors who continuously improve its libraries and frameworks. This means better documentation, extensive tutorials, and active forums where MAS developers can find solutions to common challenges.

Additionally, Python's adoption in academia ensures that MAS research and real-world applications remain closely connected. Many universities and research institutions use Python to develop MAS models, making it easier for new developers to access cutting-edge innovations and contribute to the field.

Conclusion

Python is the ideal choice for developing Multi-Agent Systems due to its simplicity, vast ecosystem, and seamless integration with AI and machine learning tools. It enables rapid prototyping, supports scalable architectures, and provides powerful frameworks for agent-based modeling and reinforcement learning.

In the next section, we will explore some of the most exciting **real-world applications of MAS**, showcasing how Python-powered multi-agent systems are shaping industries such as robotics, finance, and transportation.

1.3 Key Applications and Use Cases

Multi-Agent Systems (MAS) are transforming industries by enabling intelligent, decentralized decision-making. Whether managing fleets of autonomous vehicles, optimizing financial markets, or improving disaster response, MAS provide a flexible, scalable approach to solving complex problems. The ability of multiple agents to interact, collaborate, and compete makes these systems uniquely suited for real-world applications that require adaptability and efficiency.

Revolutionizing Robotics and Automation

One of the most well-known applications of MAS is in robotics, where multiple autonomous agents—often in the form of physical robots—work together to accomplish tasks. In **warehouse automation**, for instance, robots navigate through storage facilities, picking and transporting items without centralized control. Each robot makes local decisions based on real-time data, adjusting to changes in inventory and avoiding collisions with other robots.

Similarly, in **search and rescue operations**, drone swarms can be deployed to cover large areas efficiently. Instead of relying on a single, centrally controlled drone, multiple autonomous drones coordinate their movements, adapting to environmental conditions and identifying points of interest. This decentralized approach allows for more effective disaster response, especially in unpredictable scenarios such as wildfires or collapsed buildings.

Optimizing Traffic and Transportation

In modern cities, MAS are being used to improve transportation systems by enabling **smart traffic management**. Traffic lights, autonomous vehicles, and public transportation systems can function as individual agents, communicating with each other to reduce congestion and improve efficiency. Self-driving cars, for example, can adjust their routes dynamically based on traffic flow, while smart intersections optimize signal timings to prevent bottlenecks.

Public transit systems also benefit from MAS-driven optimization. Buses and trains can adjust schedules in response to passenger demand, ensuring better resource allocation. Ride-sharing services use similar principles, where algorithms match passengers to drivers while considering factors such as route efficiency, real-time demand, and traffic conditions.

Advancing Financial and Economic Systems

Financial markets are another domain where MAS thrive. In high-frequency trading, multiple AI-driven agents analyze vast amounts of financial data, executing trades based on patterns and real-time market fluctuations. These trading bots operate in a competitive environment, adapting their strategies based on market trends and the actions of other trading agents.

MAS also play a crucial role in **supply chain management**, where distributed agents coordinate inventory levels, delivery schedules, and production planning. In a globalized economy, suppliers, manufacturers, and distributors act as independent agents, optimizing logistics while responding to unpredictable factors such as demand spikes, transportation delays, and economic shifts.

Enhancing Healthcare and Medical Research

Healthcare is increasingly benefiting from MAS-driven solutions. In **hospital resource management**, intelligent agents monitor patient admissions, bed availability, and staff allocation to improve efficiency. AI-driven systems can predict patient influx, ensuring that medical personnel and equipment are optimally distributed.

In **drug discovery**, MAS-based simulations model complex biological interactions to identify potential treatments. Instead of relying on a single AI model, multi-agent simulations replicate how different molecules interact, significantly accelerating the drug development process.

MAS also improve personalized healthcare through **AI-powered virtual assistants** that provide real-time health monitoring and recommendations. These assistants can integrate data from wearable devices, electronic health records, and external sources to offer proactive medical insights.

Improving Cybersecurity and Defense

Cybersecurity is another area where MAS prove invaluable. In threat detection, multiple AI agents monitor network traffic, identifying anomalies that could indicate cyberattacks. Unlike traditional security systems that rely on predefined rules, MAS-based approaches allow for **adaptive, decentralized threat response**, where agents communicate and adjust their strategies dynamically.

MAS are also used in **military and defense applications**, where autonomous systems collaborate to carry out surveillance, reconnaissance, and strategic planning. Swarm intelligence, inspired by natural behaviors like ant colonies and bird flocking, allows autonomous drones and robotic units to operate effectively in high-risk environments.

Shaping the Future of Smart Grids and Energy Management

The energy sector is undergoing a major transformation with the adoption of MAS-based **smart grids**. In a smart energy network, distributed agents—such as power generators, storage systems, and consumers—balance electricity supply and demand in real time. This approach enhances energy efficiency, reduces costs, and integrates renewable energy sources more effectively.

Households equipped with smart devices can act as independent agents, adjusting power consumption based on dynamic pricing. For example, smart thermostats optimize heating and cooling schedules, while intelligent appliances shift energy-intensive tasks to off-peak hours. These adjustments, coordinated across thousands of households, contribute to a more stable and sustainable power grid.

Driving AI-Powered Gaming and Simulations

Gaming is another field where MAS have made a significant impact. In modern video games, AI agents control non-player characters (NPCs), creating **more dynamic and realistic interactions**. Rather than following scripted behaviors, NPCs can adapt to player actions, forming alliances, competing for resources, or evolving strategies over time.

MAS are also used in large-scale simulations, such as urban planning and economic modeling. By simulating thousands of autonomous entities—representing individuals, businesses, or government institutions—researchers can test policies and predict societal trends before implementing them in the real world.

Conclusion

Multi-Agent Systems are reshaping industries by enabling decentralized, intelligent decision-making. Whether improving robotic automation, optimizing financial markets, or enhancing healthcare, MAS provide solutions that are scalable, adaptive, and efficient. With Python as a powerful tool for MAS development, the possibilities for real-world applications continue to expand.

In the next section, we will explore the key **Python tools and frameworks** that simplify MAS development, providing a practical foundation for building intelligent multi-agent solutions.

1.4 Overview of Python Tools and Frameworks

Building a Multi-Agent System (MAS) from scratch can be a daunting task. Agents must interact, coordinate, and sometimes compete, all while managing their environment and learning from past experiences. Fortunately, Python provides a rich ecosystem of tools and frameworks that simplify MAS development, allowing developers to focus on system design rather than low-level implementation details.

Why Python's Ecosystem Is Ideal for MAS

Python's strength lies in its vast collection of specialized libraries designed for agent-based modeling, communication, machine learning, and distributed computing. These tools enable developers to create intelligent agents, simulate complex interactions, and deploy scalable MAS solutions in real-world applications.

At the core of MAS development, we often need frameworks that handle:

- **Agent-based modeling** – Simulating agent interactions in a structured environment.
- **Communication and coordination** – Enabling agents to exchange information and make collaborative decisions.
- **Machine learning and decision-making** – Allowing agents to learn and adapt using reinforcement learning or evolutionary strategies.
- **Scalability and deployment** – Ensuring MAS can operate efficiently across distributed computing environments.

Let's explore some of the most powerful Python tools that help achieve these goals.

Agent-Based Modeling with Mesa

For those looking to simulate MAS, **Mesa** is a go-to Python framework. It provides a structured way to build agent-based models, visualize interactions, and analyze system dynamics. Researchers and developers use

Mesa to study emergent behaviors in economics, epidemiology, urban planning, and more.

Mesa simplifies MAS simulations by providing:

- **A modular agent design** – Developers can define agents with specific properties and behaviors.
- **A flexible environment** – Agents can interact with a grid, network, or free-moving space.
- **Built-in visualization tools** – Results can be displayed in real-time using interactive charts.

Imagine designing a traffic simulation where self-driving cars (agents) navigate through a smart city. With Mesa, you can model how cars adjust their speed based on traffic conditions, detect congestion, and test optimization strategies—all within a few lines of Python code.

Distributed Multi-Agent Systems with SPADE

For MAS that require real-time communication and distributed processing, **SPADE (Smart Python Agent Development Environment)** provides a robust framework. It is built on the **XMPP protocol**, which allows agents to send and receive messages asynchronously, making it ideal for applications such as **robotic swarms, IoT networks, and cybersecurity monitoring**.

What makes SPADE stand out is its ability to:

- **Create independent, networked agents** that can run on different machines.
- **Handle asynchronous messaging**, allowing agents to communicate in real time.
- **Integrate with AI models**, enabling intelligent decision-making.

A practical example is a **multi-robot system** in an industrial setting. Robots equipped with SPADE can autonomously communicate and coordinate tasks such as assembling parts or delivering materials across a factory floor.

Reinforcement Learning with Stable-Baselines3

When building MAS with adaptive agents, reinforcement learning (RL) becomes essential. **Stable-Baselines3 (SB3)** is a popular library for implementing RL algorithms, allowing agents to learn from their environment through trial and error.

Many MAS applications, such as **autonomous trading bots, competitive game AI, and robotic navigation**, rely on reinforcement learning. SB3 provides pre-implemented algorithms like **Deep Q-Networks (DQN), Proximal Policy Optimization (PPO), and Soft Actor-Critic (SAC)**, making it easy to train intelligent agents.

For example, if you're developing a **multi-agent soccer simulation**, SB3 can help train each player to pass, defend, and score goals based on learned strategies, rather than relying on pre-programmed behaviors.

Scalability with Ray

As MAS grow in complexity, handling large-scale agent interactions becomes a challenge. **Ray**, a distributed computing framework, enables parallel processing of multiple agents across CPUs and GPUs. It is especially useful for **real-time simulations, cloud-based MAS, and large-scale reinforcement learning**.

Ray's key features include:

- **Parallel execution of multiple agents**, reducing computation time.
- **Seamless integration with reinforcement learning frameworks** like RLlib.
- **Support for cloud-based MAS deployments**, enabling large-scale real-world applications.

Consider an MAS designed for **financial market simulations** with thousands of trading agents analyzing data and making decisions simultaneously. Using Ray, developers can scale the simulation across multiple machines, significantly speeding up training and testing.

Networking and Communication with Pyro4 and ZeroMQ

In many MAS applications, agents need to communicate effectively. **Pyro4** and **ZeroMQ** provide lightweight solutions for inter-agent communication.

Pyro4 is great for **remote procedure calls (RPCs)**, allowing agents to call functions on other agents as if they were local. This is particularly useful in **distributed AI systems, where different AI components need to interact seamlessly**.

ZeroMQ, on the other hand, is a high-performance messaging library that supports **asynchronous, event-driven communication**. It is widely used in MAS applications requiring real-time updates, such as **automated trading systems, drone swarms, and distributed sensor networks**.

Graph-Based MAS with NetworkX

Some MAS applications involve **network structures**, where agents are connected through relationships rather than physical proximity. **NetworkX** is a powerful Python library for working with graphs and networked systems.

It is particularly useful in:

- **Social network analysis**, where agents represent individuals interacting in an online community.
- **Supply chain modeling**, where agents (suppliers, manufacturers, distributors) optimize logistics.
- **Cybersecurity simulations**, where agents represent nodes in a network detecting threats.

By leveraging NetworkX, MAS developers can analyze agent relationships, simulate information flow, and optimize complex decision-making processes.

Conclusion

Python provides a diverse ecosystem of tools tailored for Multi-Agent Systems, covering everything from **simulation and communication to learning and scalability**. Whether you're building an agent-based model with **Mesa**, designing a distributed system with **SPADE**, training AI-powered agents with **Stable-Baselines3**, or scaling up with **Ray**, Python's frameworks simplify MAS development and accelerate real-world implementation.

In the next chapter, we'll dive into **building a simple MAS from scratch**, using Python and these powerful tools to create an intelligent, interacting system.

Chapter 2: Fundamentals of Multi-Agent Systems

Multi-Agent Systems (MAS) are at the core of modern AI-driven automation, enabling autonomous agents to work together, coordinate tasks, and solve complex problems efficiently. Whether it's self-driving cars navigating traffic, robotic swarms assembling products, or AI-powered financial markets adjusting in real-time, MAS provide the foundation for intelligent decision-making in dynamic environments.

This chapter explores the fundamental principles that govern MAS, including different agent types, architectures, communication mechanisms, decision-making strategies, and the challenges developers face when implementing these systems.

2.1 Agent Types and Architectures

Multi-Agent Systems (MAS) revolve around **agents**—autonomous entities that sense their environment, make decisions, and act upon them. But what exactly makes an agent "intelligent," and how do we structure them for effective problem-solving? This section explores different types of agents, their internal architectures, and how they function in real-world applications.

Understanding Agents in MAS

Think of an agent as an independent decision-maker. It could be as simple as a rule-based chatbot or as advanced as an autonomous drone navigating an unknown landscape. In MAS, multiple agents interact, collaborate, or compete, forming a dynamic system capable of handling complex tasks.

The way an agent processes information and interacts with others determines its **type and architecture**. Some agents are reactive, responding instantly to inputs, while others deliberate before making decisions. Some work independently, while others coordinate their actions. Designing the right architecture depends on the problem you are trying to solve.

Let's break this down with a hands-on example.

Types of Agents

1. Reactive Agents (Reflex-Based Behavior)

A reactive agent operates on a simple principle: **"If this happens, do that."** It doesn't maintain an internal model of the world but reacts to immediate inputs. A classic example is a thermostat, which turns heating on or off based on temperature readings.

Here's a Python implementation of a basic reactive agent that acts as a simple robot vacuum cleaner. It moves randomly and cleans only when it detects dirt:

```python
import random

class ReactiveVacuumAgent:
    def __init__(self):
        self.location = random.choice(["A", "B"])
        self.environment = {"A": random.choice(["Clean",
"Dirty"]), "B": random.choice(["Clean", "Dirty"])}

    def perceive(self):
        return self.environment[self.location]

    def act(self):
        if self.perceive() == "Dirty":
            print(f"Vacuuming at {self.location}")
            self.environment[self.location] = "Clean"
        else:
            self.location = "A" if self.location == "B" else
"B"
            print(f"Moving to {self.location}")

# Running the agent
agent = ReactiveVacuumAgent()
for _ in range(5):
    agent.act()
    print(agent.environment)
```

This agent blindly moves between two locations, cleaning when necessary. However, it lacks long-term planning. If both locations are clean, it still moves aimlessly—highlighting the limitations of purely reactive systems.

2. Deliberative Agents (Planning and Reasoning)

Unlike reactive agents, deliberative agents **plan their actions** rather than responding reflexively. They maintain an internal model of the environment and use reasoning to make informed decisions.

Consider a maze-solving robot that evaluates different paths before deciding which direction to move. A simple implementation using breadth-first search (BFS) would look like this:

```python
from collections import deque

class DeliberativeAgent:
    def __init__(self, maze, start, goal):
        self.maze = maze
        self.start = start
        self.goal = goal

    def find_path(self):
        queue = deque([(self.start, [self.start])])
        visited = set()

        while queue:
            (current, path) = queue.popleft()
            if current == self.goal:
                return path

            for dx, dy in [(0,1), (1,0), (0,-1), (-1,0)]:  # Right, Down, Left, Up
                next_pos = (current[0] + dx, current[1] + dy)
                if next_pos in self.maze and next_pos not in visited:
                    queue.append((next_pos, path + [next_pos]))
                    visited.add(next_pos)
        return None

# Define a simple maze as a set of walkable positions
maze = {(0,0), (0,1), (1,1), (1,2), (2,2)}
agent = DeliberativeAgent(maze, (0,0), (2,2))

print("Path found:", agent.find_path())
```

This agent **thinks ahead** before moving, ensuring it reaches the goal efficiently rather than wandering randomly.

3. Learning Agents (Adapting and Improving)

A learning agent **improves over time** by analyzing past experiences. Machine learning techniques, such as reinforcement learning (RL), allow agents to develop optimal strategies.

Let's look at an agent using Q-learning to train itself in a grid world. Instead of predefined rules, it learns the best actions through trial and error.

```python
import numpy as np
import random

class QLearningAgent:
    def __init__(self, states, actions, alpha=0.1, gamma=0.9, epsilon=0.1):
        self.q_table = np.zeros((states, actions))
        self.alpha = alpha
        self.gamma = gamma
        self.epsilon = epsilon

    def choose_action(self, state):
        if random.uniform(0, 1) < self.epsilon:
            return random.randint(0, 3)  # Explore
        return np.argmax(self.q_table[state])  # Exploit

    def update_q(self, state, action, reward, next_state):
        best_future_q = np.max(self.q_table[next_state])
        self.q_table[state, action] += self.alpha * (reward + self.gamma * best_future_q - self.q_table[state, action])

# Simulated environment with 5 states and 4 actions (up, down, left, right)
agent = QLearningAgent(5, 4)
```

Over time, this agent **learns** an optimal path rather than relying on predefined rules. Learning agents are particularly useful in **autonomous vehicles, trading bots, and adaptive game AI**.

Agent Architectures

Different problems require different agent architectures. Here are the most commonly used ones:

1. Simple Reflex Architecture

- Uses condition-action rules.
- Fast but ineffective in complex scenarios.
- Example: Thermostat, simple chatbot.

2. Goal-Based Architecture

- Makes decisions based on achieving a predefined goal.
- Requires search algorithms (e.g., BFS, A*).
- Example: Path-planning robots, self-driving cars.

3. Utility-Based Architecture

- Evaluates different actions based on utility functions.
- Example: AI in financial markets selecting the most profitable trade.

4. BDI (Belief-Desire-Intention) Architecture

- Agents have **Beliefs** (information about the environment), **Desires** (goals), and **Intentions** (actions to achieve goals).
- Example: Intelligent assistants like Siri or Alexa.

The type of agent and its architecture **directly impact how well it performs in a given task**. Reactive agents are simple but inflexible. Deliberative agents plan but require computation. Learning agents improve over time but need training. Choosing the right architecture is key to building efficient MAS.

In the next section, we'll explore **how these agents communicate and coordinate**, a crucial factor in designing collaborative AI systems.

2.2 Communication and Coordination Mechanisms

In any multi-agent system (MAS), agents need a way to **exchange information** and **coordinate their actions**. Whether it's a fleet of autonomous drones surveying an area, stock-trading bots making real-time decisions, or smart home devices working together, effective communication is the key to intelligent collaboration.

But how do agents actually **talk** to each other? How do they **agree on tasks**, **resolve conflicts**, or **coordinate their movements**? Let's dive into the mechanisms that make agent communication and coordination possible.

Why Is Communication Essential in MAS?

Imagine a soccer team where players don't talk or signal each other. The game would be chaotic, with everyone acting independently. Similarly, in MAS, without communication, agents would struggle to align their efforts, leading to inefficiency or failure.

For instance, in **self-driving cars**, vehicles need to communicate to **avoid collisions** and **optimize traffic flow**. In **warehouse robotics**, robots must coordinate **who picks up which package** to maximize efficiency. The need for communication depends on how **cooperative, competitive, or hybrid** the system is.

Types of Communication in Multi-Agent Systems

1. Direct Communication (Explicit Messaging)

In direct communication, agents **send messages** to each other in a structured way, much like emails or chat messages. This method is common in **distributed AI systems** where agents explicitly share information.

A simple example is a **master-worker** system, where one agent assigns tasks and another executes them. Let's implement a basic **message-passing** system using Python's queue module:

```python
----
import queue
import threading

class Agent:
    def __init__(self, name):
        self.name = name
        self.message_queue = queue.Queue()

    def send_message(self, recipient, message):
```

```
        recipient.message_queue.put((self.name, message))

    def receive_message(self):
        while not self.message_queue.empty():
            sender, message = self.message_queue.get()
            print(f"{self.name} received from {sender}:
{message}")

# Create agents
agent_A = Agent("Agent A")
agent_B = Agent("Agent B")

# Agent A sends a message to Agent B
agent_A.send_message(agent_B, "Hello, let's coordinate!")
agent_B.receive_message()
```

Here, Agent A **sends a message** to Agent B, which then **retrieves and processes** it. This simple approach forms the basis of many real-world **multi-agent communication protocols**.

2. Indirect Communication (Blackboard or Shared Memory)

Instead of agents directly sending messages, they can **write information to a shared space**, like a blackboard in an office. Other agents **read** from it whenever they need updates. This is useful in **robotic swarm systems**, where each robot updates its status on a shared server.

Here's an example using a **shared dictionary** as a blackboard:

```python
----
import threading
import time

blackboard = {}

def agent_writer(agent_name, data):
    blackboard[agent_name] = data
    print(f"{agent_name} updated the blackboard with:
{data}")

def agent_reader():
    while True:
        time.sleep(1)
        print("Blackboard state:", blackboard)
```

```
# Start a reader thread
reader_thread = threading.Thread(target=agent_reader,
daemon=True)
reader_thread.start()

# Agents writing to the blackboard
agent_writer("Agent X", "Task completed")
time.sleep(2)
agent_writer("Agent Y", "Requesting new task")
```

This approach ensures **scalability** because new agents can join without modifying existing communication structures. **Traffic systems, healthcare AI, and logistics networks** often use this model.

Coordination Mechanisms in MAS

Even if agents can communicate, they must **agree on what to do**. This is where coordination strategies come in.

1. Centralized Coordination (Leader-Follower Model)

A **central agent** acts as a leader, assigning tasks and managing resources. This model is used in **traffic control systems** where a central AI **manages traffic lights** based on real-time conditions.

Here's an example where a **central agent** distributes tasks among worker agents:

```python
----
class CentralCoordinator:
    def __init__(self):
        self.tasks = ["Task 1", "Task 2", "Task 3"]

    def assign_task(self, worker):
        if self.tasks:
            task = self.tasks.pop(0)
            worker.receive_task(task)

class WorkerAgent:
    def __init__(self, name):
        self.name = name

    def receive_task(self, task):
```

```
        print(f"{self.name} received: {task}")

# Creating agents
coordinator = CentralCoordinator()
worker_1 = WorkerAgent("Worker 1")
worker_2 = WorkerAgent("Worker 2")

coordinator.assign_task(worker_1)
coordinator.assign_task(worker_2)
```

This approach **ensures efficiency** but can become a **bottleneck** if the central agent fails.

---

2. Distributed Coordination (Consensus Algorithms)

In some systems, **no single agent is in charge**—agents negotiate and reach decisions collectively. This is crucial in **blockchain networks, swarm robotics, and decentralized AI**.

A common strategy is **the leader election algorithm**, where agents vote to select a leader dynamically.

```python
----
import random

class Agent:
    def __init__(self, name):
        self.name = name
        self.priority = random.randint(1, 100)  # Higher
number = greater chance of becoming leader

def elect_leader(agents):
    leader = max(agents, key=lambda agent: agent.priority)
    return leader.name

# Creating agents
agents = [Agent("A"), Agent("B"), Agent("C")]

# Electing a leader
leader = elect_leader(agents)
print(f"Leader elected: {leader}")
```

This method ensures that **if a leader fails**, a new one can be chosen dynamically. **Decentralized AI systems** and **autonomous drone fleets** use this to maintain stability.

Conflict Resolution in MAS

When multiple agents **compete for the same resource** (e.g., two drones wanting to land at the same spot), conflicts arise.

A simple solution is the **auction mechanism**, where agents **bid for resources**.

```python
----
class Agent:
    def __init__(self, name, budget):
        self.name = name
        self.budget = budget

    def bid(self, price):
        return price if price <= self.budget else 0

# Agents with different budgets
agent_1 = Agent("Agent 1", 50)
agent_2 = Agent("Agent 2", 30)

# Running an auction for a resource
bids = {"Agent 1": agent_1.bid(40), "Agent 2":
agent_2.bid(40)}
winner = max(bids, key=bids.get)

print(f"Winner of the resource: {winner}")
```

Auction mechanisms **prevent deadlocks** and **ensure fairness** in competitive environments.

Communication and coordination are the **backbone** of multi-agent systems. **Direct vs. indirect messaging, centralized vs. decentralized coordination, and conflict resolution strategies** all play a crucial role in designing intelligent agents.

In the next section, we'll explore **how agents make decisions in multi-agent environments**, introducing **game theory, negotiation, and optimization techniques**.

2.3 Decision-Making in Multi-Agent Environments

In a world where artificial agents operate together—whether in **autonomous vehicles**, **robotic swarms**, or **financial trading systems**—how do they decide what to do? Decision-making in multi-agent systems (MAS) is a fascinating challenge. Agents must assess their environment, predict the actions of others, and make choices that align with their **individual** or **collective** goals.

Unlike a single-agent AI, which makes choices in isolation, multi-agent systems introduce **complex interdependencies**. An agent's decision **influences** others and vice versa, leading to cooperation, competition, and negotiation. Let's explore the key methods that enable intelligent decision-making in MAS.

The Core Challenge: Independent vs. Collective Decision-Making

An agent in an MAS might act **independently**, optimizing its own reward, or **collaboratively**, working with others toward a shared objective. Sometimes, agents are **selfish**, and at other times, they must **compromise**.

For example, consider **self-driving cars** at an intersection. Each vehicle could either:

1. **Act selfishly**—prioritizing its own speed and ignoring others.
2. **Act collaboratively**—adapting to avoid collisions and improve overall traffic flow.

Finding the right balance requires intelligent strategies, from **game theory** to **reinforcement learning**.

Game Theory: The Science of Strategic Decision-Making

Game theory provides a mathematical framework for **decision-making** in multi-agent settings. It helps model **cooperative** and **competitive** interactions.

One of the simplest models is the **Prisoner's Dilemma**, where two agents must decide whether to **cooperate** or **defect**, knowing that their choices impact each other.

Here's how we can simulate this in Python:

```python
class Agent:
    def __init__(self, name, strategy):
        self.name = name
        self.strategy = strategy  # "cooperate" or "defect"

    def make_decision(self, opponent_choice):
        if self.strategy == "tit-for-tat":
            return opponent_choice  # Mimic opponent's last action
        return self.strategy  # Fixed choice

# Simulating a decision round
agent_A = Agent("Agent A", "cooperate")
agent_B = Agent("Agent B", "tit-for-tat")

decision_B = agent_B.make_decision("cooperate")  # First round, B cooperates
decision_A = agent_A.make_decision(decision_B)

print(f"Agent A: {decision_A}, Agent B: {decision_B}")
```

This **Tit-for-Tat** strategy mimics the opponent's last move, promoting cooperation over time. Game-theoretic approaches like this help design multi-agent systems where **trust and fairness** emerge naturally.

Markov Decision Processes (MDPs) for MAS

Many multi-agent environments are **dynamic**, where agents make decisions based on changing conditions. Markov Decision Processes (MDPs) are a mathematical tool to model this.

Each agent's decision depends on:

- **State** – The current condition of the environment.
- **Actions** – The set of possible moves the agent can make.
- **Rewards** – The benefit (or cost) of taking an action.
- **Transition probabilities** – The likelihood of moving from one state to another.

Here's a simple implementation of an agent navigating a **grid-based world** using MDP principles:

```python
----
import numpy as np

class GridWorld:
    def __init__(self, size=4):
        self.size = size
        self.state = (0, 0)  # Start position

    def step(self, action):
        x, y = self.state
        if action == "right":
            x = min(x + 1, self.size - 1)
        elif action == "down":
            y = min(y + 1, self.size - 1)

        self.state = (x, y)
        reward = 1 if self.state == (self.size - 1, self.size
- 1) else -0.1
        return self.state, reward

# Simulating an agent moving
env = GridWorld()
actions = ["right", "right", "down", "down"]

for action in actions:
    new_state, reward = env.step(action)
    print(f"Moved {action} -> New State: {new_state}, Reward:
{reward}")
```

MDPs are widely used in **robotics, autonomous driving, and reinforcement learning** to help agents learn optimal decision strategies.

Reinforcement Learning (RL) for Multi-Agent Decision-Making

Reinforcement Learning (RL) is a powerful approach where agents **learn** the best actions by interacting with the environment. Instead of following predefined rules, agents discover strategies through **trial and error**.

In **multi-agent reinforcement learning (MARL)**, multiple agents learn simultaneously, adapting to each other's behaviors. A popular method is **Q-learning**, where agents learn an optimal policy using a **Q-table**.

Here's a basic example of a **Q-learning agent** navigating a grid:

```python
import numpy as np
import random

class QLearningAgent:
    def __init__(self, actions):
        self.actions = actions
        self.q_table = {}  # Store state-action values

    def get_q_value(self, state, action):
        return self.q_table.get((state, action), 0)

    def choose_action(self, state, epsilon=0.1):
        if random.random() < epsilon:
            return random.choice(self.actions)  # Exploration
        return max(self.actions, key=lambda a:
self.get_q_value(state, a))  # Exploitation

    def update_q_table(self, state, action, reward,
next_state, alpha=0.1, gamma=0.9):
        best_next_q = max(self.get_q_value(next_state, a) for
a in self.actions)
        self.q_table[(state, action)] = (1 - alpha) *
self.get_q_value(state, action) + alpha * (reward + gamma *
best_next_q)

# Simulating an agent learning to navigate
agent = QLearningAgent(["right", "down"])
state = (0, 0)

for _ in range(10):
    action = agent.choose_action(state)
    next_state = (state[0] + (action == "right"), state[1] +
(action == "down"))
    reward = 1 if next_state == (2, 2) else -0.1  # Goal at
(2,2)
```

```
agent.update_q_table(state, action, reward, next_state)
state = next_state

print("Learned Q-values:", agent.q_table)
```

In **real-world applications**, MARL is used in **multi-robot teams, competitive AI gaming, and financial markets**.

Decision-making in MAS is **fundamentally different** from single-agent AI. Agents must navigate **uncertainty, competition, and cooperation** simultaneously.

- **Game theory** helps model strategic interactions.
- **MDPs** provide a framework for sequential decision-making.
- **Reinforcement learning** enables agents to learn from experience.

Understanding these techniques allows us to **design intelligent multi-agent systems** that are robust, adaptive, and capable of solving complex problems.

In the next section, we'll dive into the **challenges of multi-agent coordination and conflict resolution**, where we explore how agents handle disputes, negotiate, and reach agreements.

2.4 Common Challenges in Multi-Agent Systems

Multi-agent systems (MAS) are powerful, enabling intelligent agents to work together in complex environments. But, as exciting as MAS sounds, they come with unique challenges that don't exist in single-agent AI. When multiple agents interact, new problems arise—conflicts, coordination failures, and unpredictability.

Imagine designing a **fleet of delivery drones** navigating a busy city. Each drone must avoid collisions, optimize delivery routes, and adapt to unexpected obstacles. Now, scale this up to a **global trading system** where thousands of AI agents negotiate and trade in real-time. The complexity skyrockets.

Let's dive into some of the biggest challenges in MAS and explore practical ways to address them.

1. Coordination and Communication Issues

One of the toughest problems in MAS is ensuring that agents coordinate effectively. In a single-agent system, decision-making is straightforward. But when multiple agents interact, they must **exchange information** and **make decisions collectively**.

A common issue is **message congestion**—too many agents trying to communicate at once, leading to delays or lost data. In decentralized systems, there's also no single point of control, making coordination even harder.

To illustrate this, let's simulate a simple multi-agent **message-passing system** where agents share updates about their environment.

Example: Simulating Communication Between Agents

```python
----
import random
import time

class Agent:
    def __init__(self, name):
        self.name = name
        self.messages = []

    def send_message(self, receiver, message):
        print(f"{self.name} -> {receiver.name}: {message}")
        receiver.receive_message(message)

    def receive_message(self, message):
        self.messages.append(message)

# Creating agents
agent_A = Agent("A")
agent_B = Agent("B")

# Simulating communication
agent_A.send_message(agent_B, "Obstacle detected at (2,3)")
time.sleep(1)  # Simulating network delay
agent_B.send_message(agent_A, "Acknowledged, recalculating path.")

print(f"Agent B's messages: {agent_B.messages}")
```

This is a simple case, but in real-world MAS, ensuring **reliable, scalable** communication requires protocols like **publish-subscribe (Pub/Sub), distributed message queues, and decentralized consensus algorithms**.

---

2. Conflict Resolution and Decision Conflicts

When multiple agents have competing goals, **conflicts arise**. A **self-driving taxi** may want to take the shortest route, but a **traffic management AI** might need it to slow down for safety.

In competitive MAS, like stock trading bots, one agent's **gain** is another agent's **loss**, leading to adversarial behaviors. Without proper conflict resolution, MAS can become unstable or inefficient.

Example: Resolving Conflicts Using a Voting System

A common approach to managing conflicts is **consensus-based decision-making**. In this example, agents vote on the best course of action.

```python
from collections import Counter

class MultiAgentSystem:
    def __init__(self, agents):
        self.agents = agents

    def vote(self, options):
        votes = [random.choice(options) for _ in self.agents]
        decision = Counter(votes).most_common(1)[0][0]
        return decision

# Creating agents
agents = ["Agent A", "Agent B", "Agent C"]
mas = MultiAgentSystem(agents)

# Agents voting on whether to take Route 1 or Route 2
decision = mas.vote(["Route 1", "Route 2"])
print(f"Consensus decision: {decision}")
```

Consensus algorithms like **majority voting, leader election, and blockchain-based smart contracts** are essential for resolving disputes in MAS.

3. Scalability and Computational Load

As the number of agents increases, the **computational complexity** of decision-making grows exponentially. If a **small robotic team** functions well with five agents, scaling to **500 robots** becomes a different challenge altogether.

- More agents mean **more interactions**, increasing processing time.
- Resource constraints like **memory, bandwidth, and CPU cycles** become bottlenecks.
- Synchronization across agents requires **distributed computing techniques**.

One practical approach is **hierarchical MAS**, where agents are grouped into teams, each with its own leader, reducing computational overhead.

Example: Hierarchical Decision-Making for Load Balancing

```python
----
class LeaderAgent:
    def __init__(self, name):
        self.name = name
        self.team = []

    def assign_task(self, agent, task):
        print(f"Leader {self.name} assigns {task} to
{agent.name}")
        agent.execute_task(task)

class WorkerAgent:
    def __init__(self, name):
        self.name = name

    def execute_task(self, task):
        print(f"{self.name} executing {task}")

# Creating agents
leader = LeaderAgent("Leader 1")
worker1 = WorkerAgent("Worker A")
worker2 = WorkerAgent("Worker B")

# Assigning tasks
leader.assign_task(worker1, "Patrol Area")
leader.assign_task(worker2, "Monitor Traffic")
```

Hierarchical approaches like this reduce **computational overhead** by distributing decisions rather than overloading a single system.

---

4. Security Threats and Malicious Agents

In open multi-agent environments, security is a major concern. **Malicious agents** can disrupt communication, send false information, or even take control of critical systems. This is particularly dangerous in **financial AI trading, cybersecurity systems, and autonomous warfare**.

Common security challenges include:

- **Byzantine failures**, where agents provide conflicting information.
- **Eavesdropping and message tampering**, compromising communication.
- **Adversarial attacks**, where agents are manipulated into making poor decisions.

A simple way to enhance security is through **cryptographic authentication**, where agents verify messages before acting on them.

Example: Secure Message Authentication

```python
----
import hashlib

class SecureAgent:
    def __init__(self, name):
        self.name = name

    def send_secure_message(self, receiver, message, key):
        hash_value = hashlib.sha256((message +
key).encode()).hexdigest()
        print(f"{self.name} -> {receiver.name}: {message}
[HASH: {hash_value}]")
        receiver.receive_message(message, hash_value, key)

    def receive_message(self, message, received_hash, key):
        expected_hash = hashlib.sha256((message +
key).encode()).hexdigest()
        if received_hash == expected_hash:
            print(f"{self.name} verified message integrity.")
        else:
            print(f"{self.name} detected tampering!")
```

```
# Creating secure agents
agent_X = SecureAgent("X")
agent_Y = SecureAgent("Y")

# Sending a secure message
secret_key = "shared_secret"
agent_X.send_secure_message(agent_Y, "Update position to
(4,5)", secret_key)
```

By adding **hash-based verification**, agents can **detect tampering** and ensure message integrity.

Final Thoughts

Multi-agent systems are powerful, but they introduce **new challenges** that don't exist in single-agent AI. Coordination, conflict resolution, scalability, and security are all hurdles that must be overcome.

- **Smart communication protocols** prevent bottlenecks.
- **Consensus mechanisms** help resolve decision conflicts.
- **Hierarchical designs** improve scalability.
- **Security layers** protect against malicious agents.

As MAS continue to evolve, innovations in **blockchain, federated learning, and decentralized AI** are making these challenges **easier to manage**.

Chapter 3: Setting Up the Development Environment

Before diving into building intelligent multi-agent systems (MAS), we need to set up a solid foundation. This chapter walks you through **installing Python**, **choosing the right frameworks**, and **writing your first simple agent**.

Think of it like setting up a robotics lab. Without the right tools, even the most brilliant designs won't come to life. MAS is no different—we need the right software stack to build, test, and deploy intelligent agents efficiently.

3.1 Installing Python and Essential Libraries

Before building intelligent multi-agent systems (MAS), we need a solid development environment. Think of it as preparing a workspace before assembling a team of robots. Without the right tools, even the most advanced AI agents won't function properly.

This section will guide you through installing Python, setting up a clean working environment, and installing key libraries that simplify MAS development. By the end, you'll have everything ready to start coding intelligent agents.

Installing Python

Python is the backbone of MAS development, thanks to its ease of use and the vast ecosystem of libraries available. First, check if you already have Python installed:

```sh
----
python --version
or
sh
----
python3 --version
```

If Python isn't installed or you need an update, download the latest version from python.org. During installation, check the box **"Add Python to PATH"** to ensure you can run Python from the command line.

After installation, confirm everything is working:

```sh
python --version
```

If it prints the installed version (e.g., Python 3.11.2), you're good to go.

Setting Up a Virtual Environment

A virtual environment helps keep projects clean by isolating dependencies. Imagine building multiple AI projects—one may use an older library version, while another needs the latest updates. A virtual environment ensures they don't interfere with each other.

Create a new environment:

```sh
python -m venv mas_env
```

Activate it:

- **Windows**:

```sh
mas_env\Scripts\activate
```

- **Mac/Linux**:

```sh
source mas_env/bin/activate
```

Once activated, you'll see (mas_env) before your terminal prompt, indicating you're working inside the virtual environment.

To deactivate the environment when you're done:

```sh
deactivate
```

Now let's install the essential libraries.

Installing Core MAS Libraries

Python offers powerful libraries for MAS development, handling everything from agent modeling to communication. The two major frameworks we'll work with are **Mesa** and **SPADE**.

- **Mesa** – Ideal for building and simulating multi-agent models.
- **SPADE** – Used for real-world MAS, enabling agents to communicate over networks.

Install both along with other useful dependencies:

```sh
pip install mesa spade networkx numpy matplotlib
```

Here's what each package does:

- **Mesa**: Provides an intuitive way to model and simulate multi-agent systems.
- **SPADE**: Enables agents to exchange messages asynchronously, perfect for distributed AI.
- **NetworkX**: Helps structure and analyze agent relationships using graphs.
- **NumPy & Matplotlib**: Useful for processing data and visualizing agent behaviors.

After installation, verify the libraries are installed correctly:

```sh
python -c "import mesa, spade, networkx, numpy, matplotlib;
print('All libraries installed successfully!')"
```

If you see the success message, you're ready to start coding.

Testing the Setup with a Simple Script

Let's ensure everything works by creating a simple **MAS simulation** using Mesa. The following script defines a basic agent that moves randomly on a 5x5 grid.

1. Create a new Python file (`test_mas.py`)

```python
from mesa import Agent, Model
from mesa.space import MultiGrid
from mesa.time import RandomActivation

class TestAgent(Agent):
    def __init__(self, unique_id, model):
        super().__init__(unique_id, model)

    def step(self):
        new_position =
(self.random.randrange(self.model.grid.width),
self.random.randrange(self.model.grid.height))
        self.model.grid.move_agent(self, new_position)
        print(f"Agent {self.unique_id} moved to
{new_position}")

class TestModel(Model):
    def __init__(self, width, height, num_agents):
        self.grid = MultiGrid(width, height, True)
        self.schedule = RandomActivation(self)

        for i in range(num_agents):
            agent = TestAgent(i, self)
            self.schedule.add(agent)
            self.grid.place_agent(agent,
(self.random.randrange(width),
self.random.randrange(height)))

    def step(self):
        self.schedule.step()

# Running the test
if __name__ == "__main__":
    model = TestModel(5, 5, 3)
    for _ in range(5):
        model.step()
```

2. Run the script

```sh
----
python test_mas.py
```

If everything is set up correctly, you'll see agents moving randomly in the console. This confirms that Python, the MAS libraries, and your development environment are ready.

With Python installed, a virtual environment set up, and the essential MAS libraries ready, you're now prepared to build intelligent agents. In the next section, we'll explore the different MAS frameworks in more detail, helping you choose the right tools for your projects.

3.2 Introduction to MAS Frameworks (Mesa, SPADE, etc.)

Building multi-agent systems (MAS) is much easier when you have the right tools. Instead of coding everything from scratch—defining agents, managing their interactions, and handling communication—you can use specialized frameworks that simplify the process. In this section, we'll explore two of the most widely used Python frameworks for MAS: **Mesa** and **SPADE**.

By the end of this section, you'll understand when and how to use these frameworks and implement a simple example to get started.

Why Use MAS Frameworks?

Imagine you're developing a MAS for traffic simulation. You need multiple agents (cars) navigating roads, interacting with signals, and making real-time decisions. Without a framework, you'd have to manually code agent behaviors, track movements, and optimize performance. MAS frameworks provide prebuilt tools for agent modeling, environment management, and even visualization, allowing you to focus on the logic rather than the low-level implementation details.

Let's break down two of the most useful frameworks:

Mesa: Agent-Based Simulation for Research and Prototyping

Mesa is a powerful framework designed for modeling and simulating agent-based systems. It provides built-in support for grid-based environments, scheduling mechanisms for agent actions, and visualization tools to monitor agent interactions in real-time.

Mesa is ideal for:

- Simulating complex systems like traffic flow, market dynamics, or social interactions.
- Research applications where visualization and analysis of agent behaviors are essential.
- Rapid prototyping of MAS models with structured, scalable code.

Installing Mesa

Before using Mesa, install it with:

```sh
pip install mesa
```

Creating a Simple Agent Simulation in Mesa

Let's implement a basic MAS where multiple agents move randomly in a grid.

1. **Define the agent class**

```python
from mesa import Agent, Model
from mesa.space import MultiGrid
from mesa.time import RandomActivation

class RandomAgent(Agent):
    def __init__(self, unique_id, model):
        super().__init__(unique_id, model)

    def step(self):
```

```
        new_position =
(self.random.randrange(self.model.grid.width),
self.random.randrange(self.model.grid.height))
        self.model.grid.move_agent(self, new_position)
        print(f"Agent {self.unique_id} moved to
{new_position}")
```

2. Define the model to manage agents

```python
----
class RandomModel(Model):
    def __init__(self, width, height, num_agents):
        self.grid = MultiGrid(width, height, True)
        self.schedule = RandomActivation(self)

        for i in range(num_agents):
            agent = RandomAgent(i, self)
            self.schedule.add(agent)
            self.grid.place_agent(agent,
(self.random.randrange(width),
self.random.randrange(height)))

    def step(self):
        self.schedule.step()
```

3. Run the model

```python
----
if __name__ == "__main__":
    model = RandomModel(5, 5, 3)
    for _ in range(5):
        model.step()
```

This code creates three agents that move randomly in a 5x5 grid. Each agent's movement is printed to the console.

SPADE: A Framework for Distributed Multi-Agent Systems

While Mesa is great for simulation, SPADE focuses on real-world MAS applications where agents need to **communicate over a network**. SPADE uses the **XMPP protocol**, allowing agents to interact asynchronously, making it ideal for applications like:

- **Smart cities** (e.g., intelligent traffic systems where vehicles exchange data).
- **Industrial automation** (e.g., robots coordinating in a factory).
- **AI-powered chatbots** that work together to provide information.

Installing SPADE

Since SPADE uses XMPP, we need a messaging server. For testing, we can use Ejabberd or Prosody.

To install SPADE, run:

```sh
----
pip install spade
```

Creating a Simple Agent Communication Model in SPADE

Here's how to create two agents that send messages to each other.

1. **Define the sender agent**

```python
----
import asyncio
from spade.agent import Agent
from spade.behaviour import OneShotBehaviour
from spade.message import Message

class SenderAgent(Agent):
    class SendBehav(OneShotBehaviour):
        async def run(self):
            msg = Message(to="receiver@localhost")  # Replace
with actual receiver JID
            msg.body = "Hello from SenderAgent!"
            await self.send(msg)
            print("Message sent!")

    async def setup(self):
        print(f"SenderAgent {self.jid} started.")
        self.add_behaviour(self.SendBehav())
```

2. **Define the receiver agent**

```python
----
from spade.agent import Agent
from spade.behaviour import CyclicBehaviour
```

```
class ReceiverAgent(Agent):
    class RecvBehav(CyclicBehaviour):
        async def run(self):
            msg = await self.receive(timeout=10)
            if msg:
                print(f"Received message: {msg.body}")

    async def setup(self):
        print(f"ReceiverAgent {self.jid} started.")
        self.add_behaviour(self.RecvBehav())
```

3. **Run the agents**

```python
----
if __name__ == "__main__":
    sender = SenderAgent("sender@localhost", "password")
    receiver = ReceiverAgent("receiver@localhost",
"password")

    receiver.start()
    sender.start()

    asyncio.run(asyncio.sleep(5))
    sender.stop()
    receiver.stop()
```

This script sets up two agents on an XMPP server:

- **SenderAgent** sends a message.
- **ReceiverAgent** listens and prints received messages.

To run this, you'll need an **XMPP server** (like Ejabberd or Prosody) with user accounts created.

Choosing Between Mesa and SPADE

- **Use Mesa** when you want to simulate **large-scale agent interactions** in a controlled environment (e.g., social behavior modeling, economic simulations).
- **Use SPADE** when you need agents to **communicate over a network** in real-time (e.g., smart IoT systems, multi-robot coordination).

Both frameworks are powerful and can even be **combined** for hybrid MAS solutions—such as simulating traffic flow with Mesa while allowing real-world connected vehicles to interact using SPADE.

Multi-agent systems can range from simple simulations to real-world distributed AI. Choosing the right framework makes a significant difference in implementation complexity and scalability. Now that we've explored Mesa and SPADE, the next step is to **build your first agent** and start experimenting with MAS in Python.

3.3 Writing Your First Simple Agent

So far, we've explored what multi-agent systems (MAS) are and the tools available to build them. Now, it's time to get hands-on and create your first agent in Python. This will be a simple yet functional agent that can act independently within an environment.

Agents are at the core of MAS—they perceive their surroundings, make decisions, and take actions. To get started, we'll use **Mesa**, a framework designed for agent-based modeling. By the end of this section, you'll have a working agent that moves randomly in a grid environment.

Defining an Agent in Python

In a multi-agent system, an **agent** is simply an entity that interacts with an environment and other agents. It could be anything—a person in a crowd simulation, a car in a traffic system, or even a drone in a delivery network.

Let's create a simple agent that moves around a 5x5 grid at random. We'll break this down step by step.

Step 1: Install Mesa

Before writing any code, install the Mesa framework if you haven't already:

```sh
pip install mesa
```

Mesa provides a structured way to define agents, manage environments, and run simulations.

Step 2: Create a Basic Agent Class

An agent in Mesa is a Python class that extends `mesa.Agent`. Each agent gets a **unique ID** and belongs to a **model** (which represents the simulation environment).

Here's how to define a simple agent that moves randomly:

```python
from mesa import Agent

class RandomAgent(Agent):
    def __init__(self, unique_id, model):
        super().__init__(unique_id, model)

    def step(self):
        """Defines what the agent does in one step of the simulation."""
        new_position =
(self.random.randrange(self.model.grid.width),
self.random.randrange(self.model.grid.height))
        self.model.grid.move_agent(self, new_position)
        print(f"Agent {self.unique_id} moved to
{new_position}")
```

Breaking It Down:

- The `__init__` method assigns a **unique ID** to the agent and links it to a model.
- The step method defines how the agent behaves—here, it picks a random position in the grid and moves there.

Right now, this agent exists only as a class definition. To make it useful, we need an environment where it can operate.

Step 3: Create an Environment (Model Class)

In Mesa, an environment is represented by a **Model** class. This manages agents and updates them over time.

Let's define a simple environment that holds multiple agents on a grid:

```python
from mesa import Model
from mesa.space import MultiGrid
from mesa.time import RandomActivation

class RandomModel(Model):
    def __init__(self, width, height, num_agents):
        self.grid = MultiGrid(width, height, torus=True)
        self.schedule = RandomActivation(self)

        # Create agents and place them in random positions
        for i in range(num_agents):
            agent = RandomAgent(i, self)
            self.schedule.add(agent)
            x, y = self.random.randrange(width),
self.random.randrange(height)
            self.grid.place_agent(agent, (x, y))

    def step(self):
        """Advances the model by one step, updating all
agents."""
        self.schedule.step()
```

What's Happening Here?

- `MultiGrid` creates a 2D grid where agents can move. The `torus=True` setting allows agents to "wrap around" if they move off the edge.
- `RandomActivation` schedules agents in a random order each step.
- The `__init__` method initializes the grid and creates agents, placing them in random positions.
- The `step` function moves all agents once per simulation step.

Step 4: Running the Simulation

Now, let's create a script to run the simulation and watch our agents move:

```python
----
if __name__ == "__main__":
    model = RandomModel(5, 5, 3)  # 5x5 grid with 3 agents

    for i in range(5):  # Run for 5 steps
        print(f"Step {i+1}:")
        model.step()
```

When you run this script, you'll see the agents move randomly in the grid, with their new positions printed at each step.

Step 5: Visualizing the Agents (Optional)

While text-based output is useful, seeing agent movement visually can make debugging easier. Mesa provides a simple way to create an interactive visualization.

First, install **Matplotlib** if you haven't already:

```sh
----
pip install matplotlib
```

Now, add this visualization function to your script:

```python
----
import matplotlib.pyplot as plt

def plot_agents(model):
    grid_size = model.grid.width
    agent_positions = [(agent.pos[0], agent.pos[1]) for agent
in model.schedule.agents]

    plt.figure(figsize=(5, 5))
    plt.xlim(-1, grid_size)
    plt.ylim(-1, grid_size)

    for x, y in agent_positions:
        plt.scatter(x, y, c='blue', s=100)
```

```
    plt.grid()
    plt.show()

# Run the simulation and visualize
if __name__ == "__main__":
    model = RandomModel(5, 5, 3)

    for i in range(5):
        model.step()
        plot_agents(model)
```

Now, after each simulation step, you'll see a plot displaying the agents' new positions.

Final Thoughts

You've just built a simple **multi-agent simulation** where agents move randomly in a 2D grid. While this is a basic example, the core concepts— **defining agents, creating an environment, and running a simulation**— apply to more complex systems.

In the next chapters, we'll explore:

- More advanced agent behaviors (goal-driven actions, decision-making).
- Agent communication and coordination strategies.
- Real-world applications like **swarm robotics** and **intelligent traffic systems**.

Now that you've written your first agent, you have the foundation to build **more intelligent, interactive, and scalable multi-agent systems**.

Chapter 4: Designing and Implementing Agents

So far, we've covered the fundamentals of multi-agent systems (MAS), explored agent architectures, and built a simple agent. Now, it's time to **design and implement more intelligent agents**.

In this chapter, we'll explore different types of agents, ranging from **rule-based and heuristic agents** to **learning-based agents**. We'll also dive into **multi-agent communication**, an essential capability that allows agents to collaborate effectively.

By the end of this chapter, you'll not only understand how to design different kinds of agents but also how to implement them in Python with practical examples.

4.1 Rule-Based and Heuristic Agents

Multi-agent systems (MAS) can vary from simple rule-following agents to complex AI-driven entities. **Rule-based and heuristic agents** fall into the simpler category—they don't learn or adapt dynamically but are effective for structured tasks where decision-making follows clear logic.

Think about a **traffic light system**. The lights switch based on a fixed schedule, following predefined rules. This is a rule-based system. Now, consider an **elevator**: It doesn't just follow a strict schedule but optimizes its movements based on passenger requests—a heuristic approach. Both are examples of agents that work without AI learning but can still perform efficiently.

In this section, we'll explore how to implement **rule-based** and **heuristic** agents in Python and discuss when they are useful.

Understanding Rule-Based Agents

A **rule-based agent** follows predefined **if-then** rules to determine its actions. These rules don't change over time, and the agent's behavior is entirely dictated by the logic encoded into it.

Let's take an example: a **robot vacuum cleaner**. If it detects dirt, it cleans. If it bumps into a wall, it turns. This decision-making process is entirely based on **fixed conditions** rather than learning from experience.

Implementing a Rule-Based Agent in Python

We'll create a **simple vacuum-cleaning agent** that follows rules to navigate and clean a 5x5 grid. We'll use the **Mesa** framework to simulate its environment.

Step 1: Install Mesa

If you haven't installed it yet, use:

```sh
pip install mesa
```

Step 2: Define the Rule-Based Agent

```python
from mesa import Agent

class VacuumAgent(Agent):
    def __init__(self, unique_id, model):
        super().__init__(unique_id, model)

    def step(self):
        """Defines the agent's behavior at each time step."""
        dirt = self.model.grid.get_cell_list_contents([self.pos])

        if "Dirt" in dirt:
            print(f"Agent {self.unique_id} cleaned dirt at {self.pos}")
```

```
            self.model.grid.remove_agent(self, "Dirt")   #
Remove dirt
        else:
            self.move_randomly()

    def move_randomly(self):
        """Moves to a random neighboring cell."""
        possible_moves =
self.model.grid.get_neighborhood(self.pos, moore=True,
include_center=False)
        new_position = self.random.choice(possible_moves)
        self.model.grid.move_agent(self, new_position)
```

Here, the agent **checks if there's dirt in its location**. If there is, it cleans. If not, it moves randomly.

Step 3: Create the Environment

The vacuum agent needs a **grid world** to operate in, along with dirt scattered randomly.

```python
----
from mesa import Model
from mesa.space import MultiGrid
from mesa.time import RandomActivation

class VacuumModel(Model):
    def __init__(self, width, height, num_agents):
        self.grid = MultiGrid(width, height, torus=False)
        self.schedule = RandomActivation(self)

        # Add agents to the grid
        for i in range(num_agents):
            agent = VacuumAgent(i, self)
            self.schedule.add(agent)
            self.grid.place_agent(agent,
(self.random.randrange(width),
self.random.randrange(height)))

        # Scatter dirt in random locations
        for _ in range(5):
            x, y = self.random.randrange(width),
self.random.randrange(height)
            self.grid.place_agent("Dirt", (x, y))

    def step(self):
```

```
        """Advance the model one step."""
        self.schedule.step()
```

Step 4: Running the Simulation

```python
----
if __name__ == "__main__":
    model = VacuumModel(5, 5, 2)

    for i in range(5):
        print(f"Step {i+1}:")
        model.step()
```

At each step, the agents will **check for dirt and clean** or **move randomly**. This approach is simple yet effective for structured tasks.

Understanding Heuristic Agents

A **heuristic agent** is similar to a rule-based agent but makes **more optimized** decisions based on experience or predefined strategies. Unlike strict rule-following, it may use **estimations or priority-based logic** to improve performance.

For example, **an elevator system** follows rules, but it doesn't just move one floor at a time. It prioritizes requests in the most efficient order, reducing wait times.

A good way to illustrate heuristic-based agents is **pathfinding**. Let's implement a **maze-solving agent** that follows a heuristic to find the best path.

Implementing a Heuristic Agent: Maze Solver

We'll use *A (A-star) search**, a well-known **heuristic pathfinding algorithm**, to guide the agent efficiently.

Step 1: Install Dependencies

```sh
pip install networkx numpy
```

Step 2: Define the Maze Environment

We'll create a grid-based maze where the agent must find the shortest path to the goal.

```python
import numpy as np
import networkx as nx

class Maze:
    def __init__(self, size):
        self.size = size
        self.grid = np.zeros((size, size))
        self.start = (0, 0)
        self.goal = (size-1, size-1)

    def add_obstacles(self, obstacles):
        for obs in obstacles:
            self.grid[obs] = 1  # Mark obstacles in the grid

    def is_valid(self, pos):
        """Check if the position is within bounds and not an obstacle."""
        x, y = pos
        return 0 <= x < self.size and 0 <= y < self.size and self.grid[pos] == 0
```

Step 3: Implement A Pathfinding Heuristic*

The A* algorithm selects the **most optimal path** by evaluating both the **cost so far** and the **estimated remaining cost** to the goal.

```python
from heapq import heappush, heappop

def heuristic(a, b):
    """Manhattan distance heuristic function."""
    return abs(a[0] - b[0]) + abs(a[1] - b[1])
```

```python
def astar_search(maze):
    """Finds the optimal path from start to goal using A*."""
    start, goal = maze.start, maze.goal
    open_list = []
    heappush(open_list, (0, start))
    came_from = {}
    cost_so_far = {start: 0}

    while open_list:
        _, current = heappop(open_list)

        if current == goal:
            break  # Found the goal

        for dx, dy in [(0,1), (1,0), (0,-1), (-1,0)]:  # Move
directions
            next_pos = (current[0] + dx, current[1] + dy)
            if maze.is_valid(next_pos):
                new_cost = cost_so_far[current] + 1
                if next_pos not in cost_so_far or new_cost <
cost_so_far[next_pos]:
                    cost_so_far[next_pos] = new_cost
                    priority = new_cost + heuristic(next_pos,
goal)
                    heappush(open_list, (priority, next_pos))
                    came_from[next_pos] = current

    return came_from  # Returns the path history
```

Step 4: Run the Heuristic Agent

```python
python
----
maze = Maze(5)
maze.add_obstacles([(2,2), (1,3), (3,1)])  # Adding obstacles

path = astar_search(maze)
print("Path found:", path)
```

Here, our agent **doesn't just move randomly**—it uses a **heuristic function** to intelligently choose the best path.

Rule-based and heuristic agents may not be as flexible as learning-based agents, but they are **efficient, explainable, and effective** in structured environments. While **rule-based** agents follow strict conditions, **heuristic** agents optimize their actions for better performance.

As we move forward, we'll explore how **learning-based agents** can **adapt and improve** their decisions over time.

4.2 Learning-Based Agents (Reinforcement Learning, Evolutionary Algorithms)

Multi-agent systems become significantly more powerful when agents can **learn from experience** rather than relying on static rules or heuristics. **Learning-based agents** improve their decision-making over time, adapting to dynamic environments and optimizing their strategies.

This chapter explores two major approaches:

- **Reinforcement Learning (RL):** Agents learn by interacting with an environment and receiving rewards for beneficial actions.
- **Evolutionary Algorithms (EA):** Inspired by natural selection, these algorithms evolve populations of agents over multiple generations to optimize behavior.

We'll implement **a reinforcement learning agent** and **an evolutionary agent**, demonstrating how these techniques can create adaptive, intelligent systems.

Reinforcement Learning Agents

Reinforcement learning is based on an agent making decisions, receiving feedback (rewards), and adjusting its actions to maximize long-term benefits. Think of a **self-driving car**—it tries different speeds, turns, and braking strategies, learning what keeps it on the road safely.

A **Q-learning agent** is one of the simplest RL agents. It maintains a **Q-table**, which maps **states** to **actions**, adjusting values based on rewards received. Over time, it discovers the best strategy for maximizing rewards.

Implementing a Q-Learning Agent

We'll train a simple agent to **navigate a grid world** while avoiding obstacles and reaching a goal.

Step 1: Install Dependencies

```sh
pip install numpy gym
```

Step 2: Define the Environment

We'll use a **5x5 grid**, where the agent must find the shortest path to the goal while avoiding obstacles.

```python
import numpy as np
import random

class GridWorld:
    def __init__(self, size=5):
        self.size = size
        self.agent_pos = (0, 0)
        self.goal = (size-1, size-1)
        self.obstacles = [(1,1), (2,3), (3,2)]

    def reset(self):
        self.agent_pos = (0, 0)
        return self.agent_pos

    def step(self, action):
        x, y = self.agent_pos
        if action == 0:    # Up
            x = max(x - 1, 0)
        elif action == 1:    # Down
            x = min(x + 1, self.size - 1)
        elif action == 2:    # Left
            y = max(y - 1, 0)
        elif action == 3:    # Right
            y = min(y + 1, self.size - 1)

        new_pos = (x, y)

        if new_pos in self.obstacles:
            reward = -5  # Penalize hitting obstacles
```

```
elif new_pos == self.goal:
    reward = 10  # Reward reaching the goal
else:
    reward = -1  # Small penalty for each step

self.agent_pos = new_pos
return new_pos, reward
```

Step 3: Implement Q-Learning

We use a **Q-table** (state-action mapping) and update it based on rewards.

```python
----
class QLearningAgent:
    def __init__(self, env, alpha=0.1, gamma=0.9,
epsilon=0.1):
        self.env = env
        self.alpha = alpha  # Learning rate
        self.gamma = gamma  # Discount factor
        self.epsilon = epsilon  # Exploration rate
        self.q_table = np.zeros((env.size, env.size, 4))  #
Q-values for all states and actions

    def choose_action(self, state):
        """Epsilon-greedy policy: Explore with probability
epsilon, otherwise exploit."""
        if random.uniform(0, 1) < self.epsilon:
            return random.choice([0, 1, 2, 3])  # Random
action
        x, y = state
        return np.argmax(self.q_table[x, y])  # Best action
from Q-table

    def update_q_value(self, state, action, reward,
next_state):
        """Update Q-value using the Q-learning formula."""
        x, y = state
        nx, ny = next_state
        best_next_action = np.max(self.q_table[nx, ny])  #
Best action from next state
        self.q_table[x, y, action] = (1 - self.alpha) *
self.q_table[x, y, action] + self.alpha * (reward +
self.gamma * best_next_action)

    def train(self, episodes=500):
        for _ in range(episodes):
            state = self.env.reset()
            done = False
```

```
        while not done:
            action = self.choose_action(state)
            next_state, reward = self.env.step(action)
            self.update_q_value(state, action, reward,
next_state)
            if state == self.env.goal or reward == -5:   #
Stop if goal is reached or obstacle hit
                done = True
            state = next_state
```

Step 4: Train and Test the Agent

```python
----
env = GridWorld()
agent = QLearningAgent(env)

print("Training the agent...")
agent.train(1000)

print("Testing the agent...")
state = env.reset()
while state != env.goal:
    action = agent.choose_action(state)
    state, _ = env.step(action)
    print(f"Agent moved to {state}")
```

Over multiple episodes, the agent **learns an optimal path** to the goal while **avoiding obstacles**.

Evolutionary Algorithm Agents

Instead of reinforcement learning, another way to improve agents over time is **evolutionary algorithms (EA)**. These simulate **natural selection**, evolving the best-performing agents across generations.

Imagine training a **swarm of drones** to navigate through a disaster zone. Instead of programming specific rules, an **evolutionary approach** lets the best drones "survive" and pass on their successful strategies.

Implementing an Evolutionary Agent

We'll evolve **agents that solve a maze**, selecting the best performers and mutating them to improve performance.

Step 1: Define the Population

```python
----
class EvolutionaryAgent:
    def __init__(self, genome_size):
        self.genome = np.random.choice([0, 1, 2, 3],
genome_size)  # Random sequence of moves
        self.fitness = 0  # How well it performs
```

Step 2: Fitness Function

```python
----
def evaluate_fitness(agent, env):
    env.reset()
    state = env.agent_pos
    for move in agent.genome:
        state, reward = env.step(move)
        if state == env.goal:
            agent.fitness += 10
            break
        agent.fitness += reward
```

Step 3: Evolution Process

```python
----
def evolve(population, env, generations=50):
    for _ in range(generations):
        for agent in population:
            evaluate_fitness(agent, env)

        population.sort(key=lambda a: a.fitness,
reverse=True)
        best_agents = population[:5]  # Select the top
performers

        # Crossover & Mutation
        new_population = []
        for _ in range(len(population)):
```

```
            parent1, parent2 = random.choice(best_agents),
random.choice(best_agents)
            child = EvolutionaryAgent(len(parent1.genome))
            crossover_point = random.randint(0,
len(parent1.genome)-1)
            child.genome[:crossover_point] =
parent1.genome[:crossover_point]
            child.genome[crossover_point:] =
parent2.genome[crossover_point:]
            if random.uniform(0, 1) < 0.1:  # 10% chance of
mutation
                child.genome[random.randint(0,
len(child.genome)-1)] = random.choice([0, 1, 2, 3])
            new_population.append(child)

        population = new_population
    return population
```

Over multiple generations, the **best agents evolve**, learning efficient paths through selection and mutation.

Reinforcement learning and evolutionary algorithms allow agents to **adapt, optimize, and improve** their behavior over time. Whether using **Q-learning** to navigate an environment or **evolutionary methods** to breed better solutions, these techniques are fundamental for **intelligent multi-agent systems**.

4.3 Implementing Multi-Agent Communication

Effective communication is the backbone of any **multi-agent system (MAS)**. Whether it's a fleet of delivery drones coordinating drop-offs or AI-powered stock traders exchanging market insights, communication enables agents to collaborate, share information, and make better decisions.

In this chapter, we'll explore **how agents communicate**, implement **message-passing**, and build a **simple MAS where agents work together** to complete a task.

Understanding Multi-Agent Communication

Multi-agent systems use various communication models, depending on how agents exchange information:

1. **Direct Communication** – Agents send messages to specific agents (like sending an email).
2. **Broadcast Communication** – Agents send messages to all other agents in the system (like a public announcement).
3. **Indirect Communication (Stigmergy)** – Agents leave signals in the environment for others to interpret (like ants leaving pheromone trails).

In many real-world applications, agents use a mix of these models. For example, **autonomous vehicles** might broadcast traffic conditions while also directly messaging nearby cars about potential collisions.

Implementing Multi-Agent Communication with SPADE

SPADE is a Python framework for developing **multi-agent systems** using the **XMPP (Extensible Messaging and Presence Protocol)**. It provides robust message-passing mechanisms, making it an excellent choice for implementing agent communication.

Step 1: Install SPADE

To get started, install SPADE:

```sh
pip install spade
```

Step 2: Setting Up Agents

We'll create two agents:

- **CoordinatorAgent** – Broadcasts a task.
- **WorkerAgent** – Listens and responds when it can complete the task.

Defining the Worker Agent

Each **WorkerAgent** listens for messages and responds when it receives a task.

```python
from spade.agent import Agent
from spade.behaviour import CyclicBehaviour
from spade.message import Message

class WorkerAgent(Agent):
    class ListenBehavior(CyclicBehaviour):
        async def run(self):
            msg = await self.receive(timeout=10)  # Wait for a message
            if msg:
                print(f"{self.agent.name} received task: {msg.body}")
                response = Message(to=str(msg.sender))
                response.body = f"Task '{msg.body}' completed by {self.agent.name}"
                await self.send(response)

    async def setup(self):
        print(f"Worker {self.name} is ready.")
        self.add_behaviour(self.ListenBehavior())
```

The **ListenBehavior** continuously listens for messages and responds when it receives one.

Defining the Coordinator Agent

The **CoordinatorAgent** assigns tasks to worker agents.

```python
from spade.agent import Agent
from spade.behaviour import OneShotBehaviour
from spade.message import Message
import asyncio

class CoordinatorAgent(Agent):
    class AssignTaskBehaviour(OneShotBehaviour):
        async def run(self):
            workers = ["worker1@jabber.com", "worker2@jabber.com"]
            for worker in workers:
```

```
            msg = Message(to=worker)
            msg.body = "Sort Dataset"
            await self.send(msg)
            print(f"Task sent to {worker}")

    async def setup(self):
        print(f"Coordinator {self.name} is assigning tasks.")
        self.add_behaviour(self.AssignTaskBehaviour())
```

The **AssignTaskBehaviour** sends a message to worker agents, instructing them to complete a task.

Step 3: Running the Agents

To run the agents, you'll need XMPP accounts for them. Modify the following script with valid Jabber/XMPP accounts:

```python
async def main():
    worker1 = WorkerAgent("worker1@jabber.com", "password")
    worker2 = WorkerAgent("worker2@jabber.com", "password")
    coordinator = CoordinatorAgent("coordinator@jabber.com",
"password")

    await worker1.start()
    await worker2.start()
    await coordinator.start()

    await asyncio.sleep(5)  # Allow time for message exchange
    await worker1.stop()
    await worker2.stop()
    await coordinator.stop()

asyncio.run(main())
```

Once the agents start, the **CoordinatorAgent** will send tasks, and the **WorkerAgents** will process them and respond.

Alternative: Using Python Multiprocessing for Simple Communication

If you don't want to set up XMPP accounts, you can implement a simpler **message-passing system** using Python's built-in **multiprocessing** library.

```python
import multiprocessing
import time

def worker(pipe):
    while True:
        task = pipe.recv()  # Receive a task
        if task == "STOP":
            break
        print(f"Worker received task: {task}")
        time.sleep(1)
        pipe.send(f"Task '{task}' completed.")

def coordinator():
    parent_conn, child_conn = multiprocessing.Pipe()
    worker_process = multiprocessing.Process(target=worker,
args=(child_conn,))
    worker_process.start()

    tasks = ["Analyze Data", "Train Model", "Generate
Report"]
    for task in tasks:
        parent_conn.send(task)
        print(f"Sent: {task}")
        print(f"Received: {parent_conn.recv()}")  # Get
response

    parent_conn.send("STOP")
    worker_process.join()

if __name__ == "__main__":
    coordinator()
```

Here, the **worker** listens for tasks via a **pipe** and responds once the task is completed. The **coordinator** sends tasks and processes responses.

Final Thoughts

Communication is essential for **effective multi-agent systems**, enabling collaboration and better decision-making. Whether using a **formal protocol like XMPP (SPADE)** or a simpler approach like **Python's multiprocessing**, implementing communication allows agents to work together efficiently.

In the next chapter, we'll explore **agent decision-making**—helping them reason, negotiate, and plan within a multi-agent environment.

Chapter 5: Coordination and Decision-Making in Multi-Agent Systems

In a multi-agent system (MAS), individual agents must **coordinate** their actions to achieve common goals while also making **autonomous decisions**. Whether it's **robot swarms**, **AI-powered trading systems**, or **self-driving cars**, coordination and decision-making are at the heart of their functionality.

This chapter explores **task allocation, swarm intelligence**, and **game theory**—all fundamental to making MAS effective and efficient. By the end, you'll have a solid understanding of how agents **distribute work, collaborate, and make strategic choices**.

5.1 Task Allocation and Resource Management in Multi-Agent Systems

Imagine a fleet of **autonomous delivery drones** operating in a city. Each drone has **limited battery life, payload capacity, and a set of locations to serve**. Assigning delivery tasks efficiently ensures that packages arrive on time, drones don't waste energy, and resources are distributed optimally.

This is the essence of **task allocation and resource management** in Multi-Agent Systems (MAS). Agents need to **divide tasks intelligently, balance workloads, and adapt to real-time changes**—whether they are robots in a warehouse, self-driving taxis, or software-based AI assistants.

In this section, we'll break down **how agents assign tasks and manage resources efficiently**, explore different **task allocation strategies**, and implement a hands-on example using Python.

Understanding Task Allocation in MAS

At its core, **task allocation** is about answering one question:

Which agent should perform which task, and when?

A good allocation strategy ensures that:

- Tasks are distributed **fairly** among agents.
- Agents are not **overloaded** while others remain idle.
- The system can **adapt dynamically** if an agent fails or a new task arrives.

Approaches to Task Allocation

There are two primary ways tasks can be assigned in MAS:

- **Centralized Task Allocation**: A **single controller** (like a dispatcher) assigns tasks to agents based on pre-defined rules. This is **fast and efficient** but creates a **single point of failure**.
- **Decentralized Task Allocation**: Agents **self-organize** and negotiate task assignments among themselves. This is **more flexible and scalable**, especially for **large, dynamic environments**.

Implementing Centralized Task Allocation

Let's start with a **simple centralized allocation** where a manager (central agent) assigns tasks to available worker agents.

Scenario

We have:

- Three worker agents: Agent1, Agent2, and Agent3.
- A list of tasks to be assigned.
- A **greedy assignment strategy**, where the first available agent gets the next task.

Python Implementation

```python
----
# Define available agents
agents = {"Agent1": True, "Agent2": True, "Agent3": True}  #
True means available

# List of tasks to assign
tasks = ["Inspect server logs", "Respond to customer
request", "Update inventory", "Process data"]
```

```
# Assign tasks in a round-robin manner
for task in tasks:
    for agent, available in agents.items():
        if available:  # Assign task to the first available
agent
            print(f"{agent} is assigned to {task}")
            agents[agent] = False  # Mark agent as busy
            break  # Move to the next task
```

What's Happening?

- The script **iterates through the list of tasks** and assigns each to the **first available agent**.
- Once an agent gets a task, it's marked as **busy** (not available).
- If all agents are busy, new tasks have to **wait until an agent becomes free**.

Limitations of This Approach

- **Not load-balanced**: Some agents might get more work than others.
- **Not scalable**: If we have hundreds of agents, checking availability for each task becomes inefficient.

Now, let's explore a more **decentralized** and intelligent approach.

Decentralized Task Allocation: The Contract Net Protocol (CNP)

In decentralized systems, **agents negotiate and bid for tasks** instead of waiting for assignments. One of the most well-known models is the **Contract Net Protocol (CNP)**.

How It Works

1. A **manager agent** (task owner) **broadcasts available tasks** to all worker agents.
2. Worker agents evaluate the task based on their **current workload** or **capabilities**.
3. Each agent **bids** for the task, offering a cost estimate (e.g., time to complete).
4. The manager **awards the task** to the best bidder.

Python Implementation

```python
----
import random

# Define tasks
tasks = ["Delivery A", "Delivery B", "Delivery C"]

# Agents with different workloads (lower is better)
agents = {
    "Drone1": random.randint(1, 10),  # Represents workload
level
    "Drone2": random.randint(1, 10),
    "Drone3": random.randint(1, 10)
}

# Task manager assigns tasks based on lowest workload
for task in tasks:
    best_agent = min(agents, key=agents.get)  # Select the
least busy agent
    print(f"{best_agent} wins the bid for {task}")
    agents[best_agent] += 1  # Increase workload
```

Why This Is Better?

- Agents **compete** for tasks, leading to more **efficient resource utilization**.
- **Dynamic adaptation**—if an agent is overloaded, others step in.
- No **single point of failure** since tasks **self-organize**.

Handling Resource Management in MAS

Beyond task allocation, agents must also **manage resources** like **bandwidth, battery life, processing power, or storage**.

Example: Load Balancing Servers in a Distributed System

Consider a set of **web servers** processing incoming requests. If one server is overloaded, new requests should be routed to a **less busy** server.

Python Implementation: Dynamic Load Balancing

```python
----
import heapq

# Define servers with current loads
servers = [(5, "Server1"), (2, "Server2"), (8, "Server3")]  #
(Load, ServerName)

# Min-heap to always get the least loaded server
heapq.heapify(servers)

# Assign a new incoming request
new_request = "Process Payment"
least_loaded_server = heapq.heappop(servers)  # Get server
with lowest load
print(f"{least_loaded_server[1]} assigned to {new_request}")

# Simulate server workload increasing
updated_load = (least_loaded_server[0] + 1,
least_loaded_server[1])
heapq.heappush(servers, updated_load)  # Add server back with
updated load
```

Why This Works?

- Ensures **equal distribution** of workloads.
- **Dynamically adjusts** as loads change over time.
- Works well for **scalable cloud computing** and **edge AI systems**.

Task allocation and resource management are at the core of **efficient multi-agent coordination**. We explored:

- **Simple centralized allocation** (good for small systems but not scalable).
- **Decentralized bidding (CNP)** for dynamic and self-organized assignment.
- **Load balancing techniques** for managing resources efficiently.

As MAS grow in complexity, these strategies become **essential for scalability**. In the next section, we'll dive deeper into **swarm intelligence and distributed decision-making**—how agents **work together to solve problems without centralized control**!

5.2 Swarm Intelligence and Distributed Systems

Imagine a swarm of **ants** searching for food. Individually, an ant is simple—it follows pheromone trails, carries food, and avoids obstacles. But **together, ants create an optimized foraging system**, finding the shortest paths, adapting to environmental changes, and coordinating **without a central leader**.

This is the essence of **Swarm Intelligence (SI)**—a field inspired by nature where **decentralized agents collaborate to solve complex problems**. When applied to Multi-Agent Systems (MAS), SI enables **distributed decision-making, fault tolerance, and adaptability**—crucial for **robotics, traffic management, AI agents, and large-scale computing**.

In this section, we'll **break down the core principles of Swarm Intelligence**, explore its connection to **distributed systems**, and implement **a simple swarm-based agent simulation in Python**.

Understanding Swarm Intelligence in MAS

Swarm Intelligence is **emergent behavior**—meaning complex patterns arise from **simple local interactions**. Instead of **a central authority controlling agents**, SI relies on:

- **Decentralized decision-making**—each agent acts autonomously but follows simple rules.
- **Self-organization**—patterns and solutions emerge without a global plan.
- **Local communication**—agents only interact with their nearest neighbors.
- **Adaptability**—the system responds dynamically to changes in the environment.

Real-World Examples of SI in Multi-Agent Systems

- **Robot swarms** for search-and-rescue missions.
- **Traffic flow optimization** using AI-driven vehicles.
- **Data clustering and optimization** in distributed computing.

Now, let's **bring these ideas to life with code**.

Implementing a Simple Swarm Simulation in Python

Let's create a **swarm of agents** that move in a 2D space, adjusting their direction based on **neighboring agents**—similar to how birds flock or fish school.

We'll use **Boid's model**, a classic swarm intelligence simulation, with three simple rules:

1. **Separation**: Avoid colliding with neighbors.
2. **Alignment**: Match the direction of nearby agents.
3. **Cohesion**: Move towards the center of the local group.

Step 1: Install Dependencies

We'll use **Pygame** for visualization. Install it if you haven't:

```sh
pip install pygame numpy
```

Step 2: Define the Agent Class

Each agent (boid) will have a **position, velocity, and simple rules** to follow.

```python
import pygame
import numpy as np

# Initialize constants
WIDTH, HEIGHT = 800, 600
NUM_AGENTS = 50
MAX_SPEED = 4
NEIGHBOR_RADIUS = 50

# Colors
BLACK, WHITE = (0, 0, 0), (255, 255, 255)

# Initialize Pygame
pygame.init()
screen = pygame.display.set_mode((WIDTH, HEIGHT))
clock = pygame.time.Clock()

class Agent:
```

```python
    def __init__(self):
        self.position = np.random.rand(2) * np.array([WIDTH,
HEIGHT])
        self.velocity = (np.random.rand(2) - 0.5) * MAX_SPEED

    def update(self, agents):
        neighbors = [a for a in agents if
np.linalg.norm(self.position - a.position) < NEIGHBOR_RADIUS
and a != self]

        if neighbors:
            # Rule 1: Alignment - Match direction with
neighbors
            avg_velocity = np.mean([a.velocity for a in
neighbors], axis=0)
            self.velocity += (avg_velocity - self.velocity) *
0.05

            # Rule 2: Cohesion - Move toward neighbors'
center
            avg_position = np.mean([a.position for a in
neighbors], axis=0)
            self.velocity += (avg_position - self.position) *
0.01

            # Rule 3: Separation - Avoid overcrowding
            for neighbor in neighbors:
                if np.linalg.norm(self.position -
neighbor.position) < 20:
                    self.velocity -= (neighbor.position -
self.position) * 0.02

        # Normalize speed
        speed = np.linalg.norm(self.velocity)
        if speed > MAX_SPEED:
            self.velocity = (self.velocity / speed) *
MAX_SPEED

        # Update position
        self.position += self.velocity

        # Boundary conditions (wrap around)
        self.position = self.position % [WIDTH, HEIGHT]
```

Step 3: Create and Run the Swarm

Now, let's initialize **multiple agents** and update them in a loop.

```python
----
# Initialize agents
agents = [Agent() for _ in range(NUM_AGENTS)]

running = True
while running:
    screen.fill(BLACK)

    for event in pygame.event.get():
        if event.type == pygame.QUIT:
            running = False

    # Update and draw agents
    for agent in agents:
        agent.update(agents)
        pygame.draw.circle(screen, WHITE,
agent.position.astype(int), 3)

    pygame.display.flip()
    clock.tick(30)   # Limit FPS

pygame.quit()
```

Breaking Down the Simulation

1. **Each agent moves autonomously** but follows simple rules for interaction.
2. **Swarm-like behavior emerges naturally**, with agents **flocking, separating, and aligning**.
3. **There is no central control**—only local interactions drive the system.

Swarm Intelligence in Distributed Systems

How SI Relates to Distributed Computing

Swarm intelligence principles are widely used in **distributed systems** like:

- **Load balancing**: AI-driven **server clusters** optimize resource allocation dynamically.
- **Packet routing in networks**: Ant Colony Optimization (ACO) helps **find the best routes** in network traffic.
- **Decentralized AI models**: Multi-agent reinforcement learning enables **robots and AI agents to learn collaboratively**.

Example: Distributed Task Execution in a Swarm

Let's say we have a set of **worker nodes** (robots, servers, or AI agents) that need to process multiple jobs. **Each worker autonomously decides** whether to accept a task based on its current load.

Python Implementation: Distributed Task Handling

```python
----
import random

class Worker:
    def __init__(self, name):
        self.name = name
        self.load = random.randint(1, 10)  # Represents
current processing load

    def accept_task(self, task_complexity):
        """ Accepts task if the workload allows """
        if self.load + task_complexity <= 15:  # Arbitrary
capacity limit
            self.load += task_complexity
            return True
        return False

# Create worker swarm
workers = [Worker(f"Worker-{i}") for i in range(5)]

# Distribute tasks
tasks = [random.randint(2, 5) for _ in range(10)]  # Task
complexities

for task in tasks:
    available_workers = [w for w in workers if
w.accept_task(task)]
    if available_workers:
        best_worker = min(available_workers, key=lambda w:
w.load)
        print(f"{best_worker.name} takes task (complexity
{task})")
    else:
        print("No available workers for task", task)
```

Swarm Intelligence provides a powerful **decentralized approach** for problem-solving in MAS. We explored:

- **How simple agent interactions lead to emergent behavior**.
- **Hands-on swarm simulation using Boid's model**.
- **Real-world applications in distributed computing and robotics**.

Swarm-based MAS is **scalable, fault-tolerant, and adaptable**—making it essential for **modern AI-driven distributed systems**. In the next section, we'll explore **game theory and negotiation strategies**, showing how agents **compete and cooperate** to maximize outcomes.

5.3 Game Theory and Negotiation Strategies

Imagine two self-driving cars approaching an intersection at the same time. Each car must decide whether to slow down or speed up. If both speed up, they crash. If both slow down, they waste time. But if one slows and the other speeds up, traffic flows smoothly.

This scenario perfectly illustrates **game theory**—the mathematical study of strategic decision-making where agents **compete or cooperate** to achieve the best possible outcome. In Multi-Agent Systems (MAS), game theory helps agents **negotiate, allocate resources, and make optimal decisions** in competitive or cooperative settings.

In this chapter, we'll explore key concepts in game theory, demonstrate negotiation strategies in MAS, and implement a **simple negotiation model** in Python.

Understanding Game Theory in MAS

Game theory revolves around **agents making rational choices** based on rewards and penalties. The key components of a game are:

- **Players (agents)** – The decision-makers in the system.
- **Actions (strategies)** – The choices available to each player.
- **Payoffs (rewards)** – The outcome based on chosen actions.
- **Rules of the game** – How interactions occur (simultaneously, turn-based, etc.).

Some real-world applications of game theory in MAS include:

- **Autonomous vehicles** negotiating lane changes.
- **Supply chain agents** optimizing resource distribution.
- **AI-powered bidding systems** competing for digital ads.

Let's start with a classic **Prisoner's Dilemma**, which illustrates how individual rationality can lead to suboptimal outcomes.

Prisoner's Dilemma: The Foundation of Strategic Decision-Making

The game involves **two prisoners** accused of a crime. They have two options:

1. **Cooperate** (stay silent).
2. **Defect** (betray the other).

The payoff matrix:

	Prisoner B: Cooperate	Prisoner B: Defect
Prisoner A: Cooperate	(-1, -1)	(-3, 0)
Prisoner A: Defect	(0, -3)	(-2, -2)

- If both cooperate, they each get **-1** (minor sentence).
- If one defects and the other cooperates, the defector **goes free (0)** while the cooperator gets **-3** (full sentence).
- If both defect, they each get **-2** (moderate sentence).

Individually, **defecting is the rational choice** (to avoid worst-case punishment), but collectively, **cooperating is better**.

Step 1: Implementing the Prisoner's Dilemma in Python

Let's simulate two agents playing multiple rounds of the Prisoner's Dilemma using different strategies.

```python
import random

class Agent:
    def __init__(self, name, strategy="tit_for_tat"):
        self.name = name
        self.strategy = strategy
        self.last_opponent_move = "Cooperate"  # Default
first move

    def decide(self):
        if self.strategy == "always_cooperate":
            return "Cooperate"
        elif self.strategy == "always_defect":
            return "Defect"
        elif self.strategy == "tit_for_tat":
            return self.last_opponent_move  # Mimic
opponent's last move
        return "Cooperate"

    def update_opponent_move(self, move):
        self.last_opponent_move = move

def play_round(agent1, agent2):
    move1 = agent1.decide()
    move2 = agent2.decide()

    # Payoff matrix
    if move1 == "Cooperate" and move2 == "Cooperate":
        payoff = (-1, -1)
    elif move1 == "Cooperate" and move2 == "Defect":
        payoff = (-3, 0)
    elif move1 == "Defect" and move2 == "Cooperate":
        payoff = (0, -3)
    else:
        payoff = (-2, -2)

    # Update opponent's last move
    agent1.update_opponent_move(move2)
    agent2.update_opponent_move(move1)

    return move1, move2, payoff
```

```
# Simulate multiple rounds
agent_a = Agent("Agent A", "tit_for_tat")
agent_b = Agent("Agent B", "always_defect")

for i in range(5):
    move_a, move_b, result = play_round(agent_a, agent_b)
    print(f"Round {i+1}: {agent_a.name} ({move_a}) vs
{agent_b.name} ({move_b}) → Payoff: {result}")
```

Observations

- The **"Tit-for-Tat"** strategy **mimics the opponent**, leading to cooperation when the other agent cooperates.
- The **"Always Defect"** strategy **dominates** against cooperators but leads to long-term penalties when playing against itself.
- In repeated games, **trust and cooperation emerge over time**, reflecting real-world negotiations.

Negotiation Strategies in Multi-Agent Systems

In MAS, negotiation involves **agents communicating, bargaining, and reaching agreements**. Some key techniques:

1. **Bargaining** – Agents offer deals and counteroffers.
2. **Auction-based negotiation** – Agents bid for resources (e.g., eBay, ad placements).
3. **Contract-net protocol** – A task is announced, and agents bid to complete it (used in distributed computing).

Let's implement a **simple automated negotiation** where two agents **bargain for a resource price**.

Step 2: Implementing Agent-Based Negotiation

Each agent starts with an **initial price** and adjusts it based on the opponent's offer.

```python
----
class NegotiatingAgent:
    def __init__(self, name, initial_offer, min_price,
max_price):
        self.name = name
        self.current_offer = initial_offer
        self.min_price = min_price
        self.max_price = max_price

    def propose(self):
        return self.current_offer

    def counter_offer(self, opponent_offer):
        if opponent_offer >= self.min_price:
            return "Accept"
        else:
            self.current_offer = max(self.min_price,
(self.current_offer + opponent_offer) // 2)
            return self.current_offer

# Initialize two agents with different price expectations
buyer = NegotiatingAgent("Buyer", 50, 30, 60)
seller = NegotiatingAgent("Seller", 80, 50, 100)

# Negotiation loop
for _ in range(5):
    offer = buyer.propose()
    print(f"{buyer.name} offers: ${offer}")

    response = seller.counter_offer(offer)
    if response == "Accept":
        print(f"{seller.name} accepts the deal at ${offer}!")
        break
    else:
        print(f"{seller.name} counters with ${response}")
        buyer.current_offer = response
```

Observations

- **If the offers are too far apart, negotiation fails**.
- **If both agents adjust incrementally, they converge to a deal**.
- **This simple model can be extended with reinforcement learning** for smarter bargaining.

Final Thoughts

Game theory provides a **structured approach** for decision-making in MAS. We explored:

- **Prisoner's Dilemma**, illustrating cooperation vs. competition.
- **Negotiation strategies**, showing how agents reach agreements.
- **Python implementations** of **strategic play and bargaining**.

In **real-world AI systems**, game theory is used for **autonomous trading, AI diplomacy, decentralized networks, and robotics coordination**. As MAS grows, mastering negotiation and strategic decision-making is crucial for building intelligent, self-organizing agents.

Chapter 6: Multi-Agent Learning and Adaptation

Intelligent agents are powerful, but what makes them truly *adaptive* is their ability to learn and improve over time. In **Multi-Agent Systems (MAS)**, agents operate in dynamic environments, interact with other agents, and must continually adjust their strategies. This chapter explores **how agents learn**, focusing on **reinforcement learning, evolutionary strategies**, and a **case study** on training agents for both **collaboration and competition**.

6.1 Reinforcement Learning for Multi-Agent Systems

Reinforcement Learning (RL) has revolutionized AI by enabling agents to **learn through trial and error** rather than relying on predefined rules. But what happens when multiple agents are learning **simultaneously** in a shared environment? Welcome to the fascinating world of **Multi-Agent Reinforcement Learning (MARL)**.

In this section, we'll explore how agents can learn **cooperatively or competitively**, discuss challenges unique to MARL, and implement **Q-learning** in a simple multi-agent scenario.

Understanding Reinforcement Learning in Multi-Agent Systems

At its core, reinforcement learning works by allowing an agent to **interact with an environment**, receive **rewards** based on its actions, and gradually **learn an optimal strategy** (policy).

However, in a **multi-agent** system, the learning process gets more complex because:

- **Agents influence each other's learning**: The environment is dynamic, as other agents are also learning and adapting.
- **Competition vs. cooperation**: Some agents might have conflicting goals (like in a competitive game), while others need to collaborate.

- **Exploration challenges**: Since multiple agents are changing the environment, it becomes harder to determine which actions lead to success.

To illustrate these ideas, let's build a **multi-agent Q-learning** example.

Implementing Multi-Agent Q-Learning

We'll simulate **two agents in a grid world** competing to reach a **goal**. Each agent will learn independently using **Q-learning**, one of the simplest and most widely used RL algorithms.

Step 1: Setting Up the Environment

We define a **5x5 grid** where two agents start from the top-left and aim for a goal at the bottom-right. They can move **up, down, left, or right**, and they receive a **reward of +10** for reaching the goal, but **-1** for each step taken.

```python
----
import numpy as np
import random

# Define the environment
GRID_SIZE = 5
GOAL_POSITION = (4, 4)

class GridEnvironment:
    def __init__(self):
        self.grid_size = GRID_SIZE
        self.goal = GOAL_POSITION

    def get_reward(self, position):
        return 10 if position == self.goal else -1   # +10 at
goal, -1 otherwise

    def is_terminal(self, position):
        return position == self.goal   # Stops when goal is
reached
```

Step 2: Creating the Q-Learning Agents

Each agent maintains a **Q-table**, which stores action values for different states. The agent learns by **choosing actions, receiving rewards, and updating the Q-table**.

```python
----
class QLearningAgent:
    def __init__(self, name, alpha=0.1, gamma=0.9,
epsilon=0.2):
        self.name = name
        self.q_table = np.zeros((GRID_SIZE, GRID_SIZE, 4))  #
Q-values for each state-action pair
        self.alpha = alpha  # Learning rate
        self.gamma = gamma  # Discount factor
        self.epsilon = epsilon  # Exploration probability
        self.position = (0, 0)  # Start position

    def choose_action(self):
        if random.uniform(0, 1) < self.epsilon:
            return random.choice(range(4))  # Explore
        return np.argmax(self.q_table[self.position])  #
Exploit

    def update_q_value(self, old_pos, action, reward,
new_pos):
        old_q = self.q_table[old_pos][action]
        future_q = np.max(self.q_table[new_pos])
        self.q_table[old_pos][action] = old_q + self.alpha *
(reward + self.gamma * future_q - old_q)

    def move(self, action):
        x, y = self.position
        if action == 0: x = max(0, x - 1)  # Up
        elif action == 1: x = min(GRID_SIZE - 1, x + 1)  #
Down
        elif action == 2: y = max(0, y - 1)  # Left
        elif action == 3: y = min(GRID_SIZE - 1, y + 1)  #
Right
        self.position = (x, y)
```

Step 3: Training the Agents

Now we simulate multiple episodes where the agents **explore, learn, and optimize their movements**.

```python
----
# Initialize agents
agent_a = QLearningAgent("Agent A")
agent_b = QLearningAgent("Agent B")

env = GridEnvironment()

# Training loop
num_episodes = 500
for episode in range(num_episodes):
    agent_a.position, agent_b.position = (0, 0), (0, 0)   #
Reset positions

    while not env.is_terminal(agent_a.position) and not
env.is_terminal(agent_b.position):
        for agent in [agent_a, agent_b]:
            old_pos = agent.position
            action = agent.choose_action()
            agent.move(action)
            reward = env.get_reward(agent.position)
            agent.update_q_value(old_pos, action, reward,
agent.position)

print("Training complete. Agents have learned optimal
paths.")
```

Key Takeaways from the Implementation

- **Agents learn independently but influence each other.** If one agent learns a **better path**, the other may adjust.
- **Exploration vs. exploitation is crucial.** If an agent doesn't explore, it may get stuck in **suboptimal behaviors**.
- **Different learning strategies yield different behaviors.** If we modify rewards, agents may choose to **block each other's path** rather than just reaching the goal.

Challenges in Multi-Agent RL

1. Non-Stationarity

In **single-agent RL**, the environment is static. But in MARL, as **one agent learns**, the environment **changes** for others. This makes learning **unstable** and harder to converge.

2. Coordination and Cooperation

If multiple agents have **similar goals**, they must **cooperate** (e.g., self-driving cars coordinating at intersections). This requires specialized strategies like **joint action learning** or **communication-based reinforcement learning**.

3. Credit Assignment

In multi-agent systems, it's **hard to determine** which agent contributed to success. This is known as the **credit assignment problem**.

4. Balancing Competition and Collaboration

Some scenarios involve both **cooperation and competition**. For example, in **soccer**, players cooperate within a team but compete against opponents.

Real-World Applications of Multi-Agent RL

- **Traffic Control Systems:** Autonomous vehicles negotiating intersections.
- **Robotics:** Swarms of drones or warehouse robots optimizing movement.
- **Finance and Trading:** Multiple AI traders interacting in financial markets.
- **Gaming:** AI-driven opponents that adapt to player behavior in games like **Dota 2 and StarCraft II**.

Multi-Agent Reinforcement Learning **adds complexity but also opens new frontiers** in AI. By **learning in dynamic environments**, agents can **compete, collaborate, and adapt** in ways that are **closer to real-world intelligence**.

In this section, we:

- Explored the basics of **MARL** and why it's challenging.
- Built a **multi-agent Q-learning system** from scratch.
- Discussed key **challenges and real-world applications**.

In the next section, we'll explore **evolutionary strategies**—another powerful method that takes inspiration from **natural selection** to optimize agent behaviors. Stay tuned!

6.2 Evolutionary Strategies and Optimization

Imagine if instead of painstakingly programming every agent's behavior, we let them **evolve**—just like natural selection shaped intelligence in the real world. This is the essence of **Evolutionary Strategies (ES)** and other optimization techniques inspired by nature. These approaches allow multi-agent systems (MAS) to adapt over time, improving their behaviors without requiring explicit rule-based programming.

In this section, we'll explore the core ideas behind **evolutionary optimization**, build a **genetic algorithm (GA) for multi-agent learning**, and discuss real-world applications of these techniques.

Why Evolutionary Strategies Matter in Multi-Agent Systems

In many **complex** environments, traditional machine learning techniques—such as reinforcement learning—struggle due to the **high dimensionality of the search space** and **non-stationary dynamics** (where agents affect each other's learning). Evolutionary strategies offer an alternative by using **population-based optimization**, meaning:

- Instead of training a **single** agent, we evolve an **entire population** of agents.
- Agents undergo **selection, mutation, and crossover**, mimicking biological evolution.
- Over generations, the population **adapts** to optimize a given objective, such as coordination, efficiency, or competition.

To see this in action, let's implement a **genetic algorithm** for evolving agent behaviors.

Implementing a Genetic Algorithm for Multi-Agent Optimization

We'll create a **swarm of agents** navigating a grid world. Each agent has a set of **genes** (movement strategies), and the best-performing ones will reproduce to form the next generation.

Step 1: Defining the Environment

Each agent starts in a **5×5 grid** and aims to reach a **goal** at the bottom-right corner. Fitness is determined by **how close the agent gets to the goal**.

```python
import numpy as np
import random

GRID_SIZE = 5
GOAL_POSITION = (4, 4)

class GridEnvironment:
    def __init__(self):
        self.grid_size = GRID_SIZE
        self.goal = GOAL_POSITION

    def get_fitness(self, position):
        return - (abs(position[0] - self.goal[0]) +
abs(position[1] - self.goal[1]))  # Manhattan distance
```

Step 2: Creating the Agent Genome

Each agent has a **genome**, which is a sequence of **actions** (0: Up, 1: Down, 2: Left, 3: Right). The goal is to **evolve better movement strategies**.

```python
class GeneticAgent:
    def __init__(self, genome_length=10):
        self.position = (0, 0)  # Start position
```

```
        self.genome = [random.randint(0, 3) for _ in
range(genome_length)]  # Random actions
        self.fitness = 0

    def move(self, action):
        x, y = self.position
        if action == 0: x = max(0, x - 1)  # Up
        elif action == 1: x = min(GRID_SIZE - 1, x + 1)  #
Down
        elif action == 2: y = max(0, y - 1)  # Left
        elif action == 3: y = min(GRID_SIZE - 1, y + 1)  #
Right
        self.position = (x, y)

    def evaluate_fitness(self, env):
        self.fitness = env.get_fitness(self.position)
```

Step 3: Evolutionary Process (Selection, Crossover, Mutation)

We evolve a **population of agents** over multiple generations. Each generation follows these steps:

1. **Selection**: Pick the best agents based on fitness.
2. **Crossover**: Combine genomes of top agents to create offspring.
3. **Mutation**: Introduce small random changes to avoid stagnation.

```python
----
def evolve_population(population, env, mutation_rate=0.1):
    # Evaluate fitness of each agent
    for agent in population:
        agent.position = (0, 0)  # Reset position
        for action in agent.genome:  # Execute genome actions
            agent.move(action)
        agent.evaluate_fitness(env)

    # Select top 50% of agents based on fitness
    population.sort(key=lambda agent: agent.fitness,
reverse=True)
    top_agents = population[:len(population)//2]

    # Generate offspring through crossover
    offspring = []
    while len(offspring) < len(population):
        parent1, parent2 = random.sample(top_agents, 2)
        crossover_point = random.randint(0,
len(parent1.genome) - 1)
```

```
        child_genome = parent1.genome[:crossover_point] +
parent2.genome[crossover_point:]

        # Apply mutation
        if random.uniform(0, 1) < mutation_rate:
            mutation_idx = random.randint(0,
len(child_genome) - 1)
            child_genome[mutation_idx] = random.randint(0, 3)

        offspring.append(GeneticAgent())
        offspring[-1].genome = child_genome

    return offspring
```

Step 4: Running the Evolutionary Process

We start with **random agents** and let them evolve over **20 generations**.

```python
----
# Initialize population
num_agents = 10
population = [GeneticAgent() for _ in range(num_agents)]
env = GridEnvironment()

# Run evolution
generations = 20
for gen in range(generations):
    population = evolve_population(population, env)
    best_fitness = max(agent.fitness for agent in population)
    print(f"Generation {gen + 1}: Best Fitness =
{best_fitness}")

print("Evolution complete! Best agents have evolved optimal
strategies.")
```

What Did We Learn from This Implementation?

- Instead of **programming** optimal behavior, we let agents **evolve** their strategies.
- The **fittest agents** (those who reach the goal faster) survive and pass their genes to the next generation.
- Over multiple generations, agents **discover better movement strategies**, even though we never explicitly told them how to navigate.

Challenges in Evolutionary Strategies for MAS

1. **Computational Cost**
   Simulating and evolving **large populations** can be expensive. Efficient parallelization helps tackle this.
2. **Difficult Reward Landscapes**
   If agents receive rewards only at the **very end** (e.g., reaching the goal), they struggle to evolve. **Intermediate rewards** help guide learning.
3. **Diversity vs. Convergence**
   If mutations are **too strong**, evolution becomes **random**. If mutations are **too weak**, the population gets stuck in **suboptimal behaviors**. Striking a balance is key.

Real-World Applications of Evolutionary Strategies

- **Robotics**: Swarms of robots learning **collision avoidance** and **path planning**.
- **Autonomous Vehicles**: Optimizing self-driving car policies using evolutionary learning.
- **Game AI**: AI opponents in games like **StarCraft II** evolving better strategies.
- **Finance**: Evolving **trading algorithms** to maximize profits in **dynamic markets**.

Evolutionary strategies provide a powerful **alternative to traditional learning** by enabling agents to **self-improve** through adaptation.

In this section, we:

- Explored **evolutionary optimization** and its role in MAS.
- Built a **genetic algorithm** for evolving multi-agent strategies.
- Discussed **challenges and real-world applications**.

Next, we'll dive into **training agents for collaboration and competition**, exploring how they learn **teamwork, negotiation, and strategic planning**. Stay tuned!

6.3 Case Study: Training Agents for Collaboration and Competition

Imagine a world where AI agents must **work together** to complete tasks—or compete against each other for limited resources. Whether it's **self-driving cars coordinating traffic**, **robots collaborating in warehouses**, or **trading bots competing in financial markets**, multi-agent systems (MAS) thrive in dynamic environments.

In this case study, we'll **train agents** to navigate a shared environment using **both collaboration and competition strategies**. By the end, you'll have a working example of **how agents learn to cooperate or compete**, and you'll understand the trade-offs between these two paradigms.

The Scenario: A Multi-Agent Grid World

Our environment is a **grid-based world** where multiple agents navigate toward **goal positions** while avoiding collisions. The twist?

- **Collaboration Mode**: Agents **work together** to maximize collective reward.
- **Competition Mode**: Agents **compete** to reach the goal first, at the expense of others.

The challenge is to train agents that can **adapt** based on their objectives.

Step 1: Setting Up the Environment

First, we define our **grid world**, where agents can move in four directions (Up, Down, Left, Right). The reward system changes based on whether agents are collaborating or competing.

```python
import numpy as np
import random
```

```
GRID_SIZE = 5
NUM_AGENTS = 2

class GridWorld:
    def __init__(self, mode="collaboration"):
        self.size = GRID_SIZE
        self.mode = mode
        self.goal_positions = [(4, 4), (0, 4)]  # Goal
positions for agents
        self.reset()

    def reset(self):
        self.agent_positions = [(0, 0), (4, 0)]  # Start
positions
        return self.agent_positions

    def move_agent(self, agent_idx, action):
        x, y = self.agent_positions[agent_idx]
        if action == 0: x = max(0, x - 1)  # Up
        elif action == 1: x = min(self.size - 1, x + 1)  #
Down
        elif action == 2: y = max(0, y - 1)  # Left
        elif action == 3: y = min(self.size - 1, y + 1)  #
Right

        self.agent_positions[agent_idx] = (x, y)

    def get_reward(self, agent_idx):
        if self.mode == "collaboration":
            return sum([-abs(pos[0] - goal[0]) - abs(pos[1] -
goal[1]) for pos, goal in zip(self.agent_positions,
self.goal_positions)])
        else:  # Competition mode
            return -abs(self.agent_positions[agent_idx][0] -
self.goal_positions[agent_idx][0]) -
abs(self.agent_positions[agent_idx][1] -
self.goal_positions[agent_idx][1])

    def is_done(self):
        return self.agent_positions == self.goal_positions
```

Step 2: Implementing Agents with Reinforcement Learning

Each agent **learns** using a simple **Q-learning algorithm**. The goal is to
maximize rewards by choosing the best actions over time.

```python
----
class QLearningAgent:
```

```python
    def __init__(self, alpha=0.1, gamma=0.9, epsilon=0.2):
        self.alpha = alpha  # Learning rate
        self.gamma = gamma  # Discount factor
        self.epsilon = epsilon  # Exploration rate
        self.q_table = {}  # Q-values stored as {(state,
action): value}

    def get_q_value(self, state, action):
        return self.q_table.get((state, action), 0.0)

    def choose_action(self, state):
        if random.uniform(0, 1) < self.epsilon:
            return random.randint(0, 3)  # Explore
        else:
            return max(range(4), key=lambda a:
self.get_q_value(state, a))  # Exploit

    def update_q_value(self, state, action, reward,
next_state):
        best_next_action = max(range(4), key=lambda a:
self.get_q_value(next_state, a))
        self.q_table[(state, action)] = (1 - self.alpha) *
self.get_q_value(state, action) + \
                                         self.alpha * (reward
+ self.gamma * self.get_q_value(next_state,
best_next_action))
```

Step 3: Training the Agents

We now train two agents, letting them **either collaborate or compete** over multiple episodes.

```python
env = GridWorld(mode="collaboration")  # Change to
"competition" to test competition mode
agents = [QLearningAgent() for _ in range(NUM_AGENTS)]

episodes = 1000

for episode in range(episodes):
    state = env.reset()

    while not env.is_done():
        actions = [agents[i].choose_action(state[i]) for i in
range(NUM_AGENTS)]
        for i, action in enumerate(actions):
            env.move_agent(i, action)
```

```
        next_state = tuple(env.agent_positions)
        rewards = [env.get_reward(i) for i in
range(NUM_AGENTS)]

        for i in range(NUM_AGENTS):
            agents[i].update_q_value(state[i], actions[i],
rewards[i], next_state[i])

        state = next_state

    if episode % 100 == 0:
        print(f"Episode {episode}: Agents' Positions
{state}")
```

Step 4: Observing Agent Behavior

After training, we analyze how agents behave:

1. **Collaboration Mode**:
   - Agents **learn to coordinate** movements to **minimize collective distance** to their goals.
   - They avoid unnecessary moves that could slow down the other agent.
   - They **maximize shared rewards** instead of individual ones.
2. **Competition Mode**:
   - Each agent **prioritizes its own goal** and doesn't care about the other.
   - If blocking an opponent improves their own reward, they do it.
   - The stronger agent reaches the goal **faster**, while the weaker agent struggles.

Key Takeaways from Collaboration vs. Competition

- **Collaboration leads to efficiency**: Agents in **cooperative** environments learn to **help each other**, improving overall success rates.
- **Competition introduces complexity**: Competitive agents sometimes **hinder each other's progress**, making learning harder.
- **Hybrid strategies work best**: In real-world MAS, **mixing collaboration and competition** leads to **more adaptable agents**.

For example, in **self-driving car networks**, vehicles must sometimes **compete for lanes** but also **cooperate** for smooth traffic flow. A fully competitive strategy would lead to congestion, while full cooperation might not always be optimal.

Final Thoughts

In this case study, we:

- Built a **grid world** for multi-agent interaction.
- Trained **Q-learning agents** to **collaborate or compete**.
- Observed how **collaborative** agents optimize for collective success, while **competitive** agents prioritize self-interest.

This example demonstrates **the importance of balancing competition and cooperation** in MAS.

In the next chapter, we'll dive deeper into **how multi-agent learning can be improved using advanced techniques** like **deep reinforcement learning**.

Chapter 7: Real-World Applications of Multi-Agent Systems

Multi-Agent Systems (MAS) are not just theoretical constructs; they **power real-world solutions** in robotics, finance, transportation, and even healthcare. Whether it's **autonomous drones coordinating deliveries, AI-powered trading bots optimizing portfolios, or traffic systems reducing congestion**, MAS plays a crucial role in shaping modern technology.

In this chapter, we'll explore how MAS is applied across different industries, showcasing real-world **problems, solutions, and hands-on implementations**.

7.1 MAS in Robotics and Autonomous Systems

When you think of robots, you might picture a single, highly intelligent machine handling a complex task. But in reality, many of the most impressive robotic applications rely on **collaborating robots** rather than a single super-intelligent one. Whether it's a team of drones surveying disaster zones, warehouse robots managing inventory, or autonomous vehicles coordinating in traffic, **multi-agent systems (MAS) play a crucial role in robotics**.

This chapter explores how **robotic agents work together**, how they **make decisions**, and how you can build a **basic multi-agent robotic simulation** to see these principles in action.

Why Multi-Agent Systems Matter in Robotics

Robotics is fundamentally about autonomy—machines making their own decisions in dynamic environments. But real-world tasks are often too complex for a single robot to handle alone. That's where MAS comes in.

Imagine a **warehouse** where hundreds of robots manage inventory. If each robot worked independently, chaos would ensue. With MAS, they **coordinate tasks, share information, and optimize efficiency**.

Some real-world examples of MAS in robotics:

- **Swarm robotics**: Groups of drones or robots that collaborate, inspired by natural systems like ant colonies.
- **Autonomous vehicles**: Self-driving cars communicating to optimize traffic flow.
- **Factory automation**: Robot arms working together to assemble products.
- **Search and rescue**: Teams of robots exploring disaster zones, covering large areas efficiently.

To see how MAS works in robotics, let's start with a **simple multi-robot system simulation**.

Building a Basic Multi-Robot Coordination System

To understand MAS in robotics, let's simulate a scenario where multiple robots explore a **grid-based environment**, searching for a target.

Step 1: Setting Up the Environment

We'll create a **grid-world** where robots move and communicate. Each robot follows simple rules:

- Move towards the target if detected.
- Share information with nearby robots.

Let's start by defining the environment:

```python
import numpy as np
import random

# Define grid size
GRID_SIZE = 10
NUM_ROBOTS = 5

class Environment:
    def __init__(self):
        self.grid = np.zeros((GRID_SIZE, GRID_SIZE))
        self.target = (random.randint(0, GRID_SIZE-1),
random.randint(0, GRID_SIZE-1))
```

```python
    def display(self, robots):
        grid_copy = np.zeros((GRID_SIZE, GRID_SIZE),
dtype=str)
        grid_copy[:] = '-'

        for r in robots:
            grid_copy[r.position] = 'R'  # Mark robot
positions

        grid_copy[self.target] = 'T'  # Mark target position
        print("\n".join([" ".join(row) for row in
grid_copy]))
        print("\n")

# Initialize environment
env = Environment()
env.display([])
```

Here, we create a **10x10 grid** with a randomly placed target.

Step 2: Defining the Robot Agents

Each robot will:

1. Move in a random direction.
2. Check if it found the target.
3. Share information with nearby robots.

```python
python
----
class Robot:
    def __init__(self, env):
        self.position = (random.randint(0, GRID_SIZE-1),
random.randint(0, GRID_SIZE-1))
        self.environment = env

    def move(self):
        x, y = self.position
        dx, dy = random.choice([(0,1), (1,0), (0,-1), (-
1,0)])  # Move randomly
        new_position = (max(0, min(GRID_SIZE-1, x+dx)),
max(0, min(GRID_SIZE-1, y+dy)))
        self.position = new_position

    def check_target(self):
        return self.position == self.environment.target
```

```
# Initialize robots
robots = [Robot(env) for _ in range(NUM_ROBOTS)]

# Simulate movement
for step in range(20):  # Run for 20 steps
    for robot in robots:
        robot.move()
        if robot.check_target():
            print(f"Target found by robot at {robot.position}
in {step} steps!")
            break
    env.display(robots)
```

How This Relates to Real-World Robotics

This simple example captures **fundamental MAS principles** in robotics:

1. **Decentralized Decision-Making**
   o Each robot acts independently, but they work toward a common goal.
2. **Communication and Coordination**
   o Robots can share target location once one finds it (in real-world systems, they'd use wireless signals or direct messaging).
3. **Adaptation in Dynamic Environments**
   o The robots adjust their movement in real-time to search the environment.

Where Do We See This in the Real World?

- **Warehouse Robots**: Similar algorithms are used in Amazon's fulfillment centers, where robots **navigate shelves** to pick and place products efficiently.
- **Drones in Agriculture**: Drones surveying large farmlands use swarm-like coordination to cover fields **without overlap**.
- **Autonomous Cars**: Self-driving vehicles use **agent-based decision-making** to navigate traffic, anticipate obstacles, and optimize routes.

Next Steps: Enhancing MAS in Robotics

We've just scratched the surface. To take MAS robotics further, you could:

- Implement **obstacle avoidance** (robots detecting and avoiding collisions).

- Introduce **multi-agent communication** (robots relaying target location).
- Use **machine learning** to make robots adapt and optimize movement patterns.

7.2 Traffic and Transportation Simulations

Managing traffic is one of the most challenging problems cities face. From congestion to accidents, inefficiencies in transportation impact millions daily. Multi-Agent Systems (MAS) offer a powerful way to simulate and optimize traffic flow, helping urban planners, engineers, and policymakers design smarter transportation networks.

In this section, we'll explore how MAS is applied in **traffic and transportation** and guide you through **building a simple traffic simulation** using Python.

Why Multi-Agent Systems in Traffic Management?

Traditional traffic control relies on **static rules**—like timed traffic lights and pre-planned routes. But real-world traffic is **dynamic**. Vehicles, pedestrians, and public transport all interact in unpredictable ways.

MAS allows **traffic systems to be modeled as collections of intelligent agents** (cars, buses, intersections, pedestrians) that make **independent** but **coordinated** decisions.

Some real-world applications include:

- **Smart Traffic Lights**: AI-controlled lights that adapt in real-time.
- **Autonomous Vehicles**: Self-driving cars communicating to prevent congestion.
- **Public Transport Optimization**: Simulating bus/train schedules for efficiency.
- **Emergency Response Routing**: Dynamic rerouting to clear paths for ambulances and fire trucks.

To see MAS in action, let's build a **simple traffic simulation** where multiple cars move along a road, avoiding collisions and optimizing speed.

Building a Simple Traffic Simulation

We'll create a **one-lane road simulation** where cars move forward, adjust speed based on traffic, and avoid collisions.

Step 1: Setting Up the Environment

We'll define a **road** as a list of cells where cars move.

```python
----
import numpy as np
import random
import time

# Define road parameters
ROAD_LENGTH = 20  # Number of positions on the road
NUM_CARS = 5  # Number of cars in simulation
MAX_SPEED = 3  # Maximum speed a car can travel

class Road:
    def __init__(self, length, num_cars):
        self.length = length
        self.road = np.full(length, None)  # Empty road
        self.cars = []

        # Place cars randomly on the road
        positions = random.sample(range(length), num_cars)
        for pos in positions:
            car = Car(pos, random.randint(1, MAX_SPEED))
            self.cars.append(car)
            self.road[pos] = car

    def display(self):
        road_display = ["-" if cell is None else "C" for cell
in self.road]
        print("".join(road_display))

# Initialize the road
road = Road(ROAD_LENGTH, NUM_CARS)
road.display()
```

Here, we create a **20-cell road** and randomly place **5 cars** with different speeds. The `display` function prints the road, showing cars as `"C"` and empty spaces as `"-"`.

Step 2: Defining the Car Agents

Each car **adjusts speed** based on the distance to the next car.

```python
----
class Car:
    def __init__(self, position, speed):
        self.position = position
        self.speed = speed

    def move(self, road):
        # Check distance to the next car
        next_car_distance = self.check_distance(road)

        # Slow down if needed
        if next_car_distance < self.speed:
            self.speed = max(1, next_car_distance)  # Avoid
collisions
        else:
            self.speed = min(self.speed + 1, MAX_SPEED)  #
Accelerate if possible

        # Update position
        new_position = (self.position + self.speed) %
ROAD_LENGTH
        road.road[self.position] = None  # Clear old position
        self.position = new_position
        road.road[self.position] = self  # Update new
position

    def check_distance(self, road):
        """Finds the distance to the next car ahead."""
        for i in range(1, ROAD_LENGTH):
            check_pos = (self.position + i) % ROAD_LENGTH
            if road.road[check_pos] is not None:
                return i  # Distance to next car
        return ROAD_LENGTH  # No car ahead

# Run simulation
for step in range(10):  # Simulate 10 time steps
    print(f"\nStep {step+1}:")
    for car in road.cars:
        car.move(road)
    road.display()
    time.sleep(1)
```

What's Happening Here?

Each **car acts as an independent agent**, making local decisions:

1. **Checking the road ahead**: The car finds the next car's position.
2. **Adjusting speed**: If the road is clear, the car **accelerates**. If traffic is heavy, it **slows down** to avoid collisions.
3. **Updating position**: The car moves forward based on its adjusted speed.

The output will show the movement of cars over 10 time steps, where cars naturally **avoid crashes and adapt speeds** dynamically.

Extending the Simulation

This basic model captures key MAS traffic principles. You can extend it by:

- **Adding traffic lights**: Simulating adaptive signal control.
- **Modeling lane changes**: Cars deciding when to switch lanes.
- **Introducing autonomous vehicles**: Simulating self-driving cars optimizing routes.
- **Adding pedestrian agents**: Simulating human movement in urban areas.

Real-World Applications of MAS in Traffic

Cities worldwide are leveraging **MAS for smarter traffic management**.

- **Smart Traffic Lights**
  Cities like Los Angeles and Singapore use AI-controlled traffic lights that **adapt based on real-time conditions**—reducing congestion.
- **Connected Autonomous Vehicles**
  Tesla and Waymo use MAS-like coordination where cars **exchange data**, making safer and more efficient decisions.
- **Public Transit Optimization**
  Transport agencies use **multi-agent simulations** to **design bus/train schedules** that optimize for demand and efficiency.

Traffic and transportation are perfect **real-world applications of MAS**. The ability of **decentralized agents (cars, traffic lights, pedestrians) to self-organize** leads to **smarter, more efficient systems**.

Our simple Python simulation already shows how cars can **adjust speeds and prevent collisions**. With further refinements—such as **AI-powered optimization**—MAS will continue to **transform modern transportation**.

7.3 AI in Finance and Market Simulations

Financial markets are complex, dynamic environments driven by countless independent agents—traders, investors, banks, and even automated trading systems. Multi-Agent Systems (MAS) provide a powerful framework for simulating and understanding these interactions, helping analysts, economists, and AI researchers **predict trends, test strategies, and optimize trading behaviors**.

In this section, we'll explore how MAS applies to **financial markets** and walk through a **simple market simulation** using Python.

Why Use MAS in Financial Markets?

Traditional financial models often assume **rational decision-making** and **predictable trends**, but real markets are far more unpredictable. MAS models financial markets as **a system of interacting agents**, each with their own **strategies, risk tolerances, and behaviors**.

This approach enables:

- **Market trend simulations**: Predicting how traders respond to economic events.
- **Algorithmic trading**: Designing AI-driven trading bots that adapt in real-time.
- **Risk analysis**: Simulating worst-case scenarios for stock crashes.
- **Behavior modeling**: Understanding how different types of traders (e.g., risk-averse vs. risk-seeking) impact the market.

Now, let's build a **basic stock market simulation** using Python.

Building a Simple Market Simulation

We'll create a **marketplace where multiple traders buy and sell a single stock** based on their individual strategies.

Step 1: Setting Up the Market Environment

We'll define a **Market** class that manages stock prices and trades.

```python
----
import numpy as np
import random
import matplotlib.pyplot as plt

class Market:
    def __init__(self, initial_price=100):
        self.price = initial_price  # Initial stock price
        self.history = [initial_price]  # Price history

    def update_price(self, trades):
        """Adjusts stock price based on supply & demand from trades."""
        total_demand = sum(trade for trade in trades if trade > 0)
        total_supply = sum(-trade for trade in trades if trade < 0)

        # Simple price adjustment: demand drives price up, supply drives it down
        if total_demand > total_supply:
            self.price *= 1 + (total_demand - total_supply) / 1000
        elif total_supply > total_demand:
            self.price *= 1 - (total_supply - total_demand) / 1000

        # Store price history
        self.history.append(self.price)

    def plot_market(self):
        """Visualizes the stock price changes over time."""
        plt.plot(self.history)
        plt.xlabel("Time Step")
        plt.ylabel("Stock Price")
        plt.title("Market Simulation")
        plt.show()
```

This creates a **basic stock market** where prices **fluctuate based on supply and demand**.

Step 2: Defining Trader Agents

Now, let's define different types of traders:

- **Random traders**: Buy/sell randomly.
- **Trend followers**: Buy when the price is rising, sell when it's falling.
- **Value investors**: Buy when the price is low, sell when it's high.

```python
----
class Trader:
    def __init__(self, strategy, cash=1000, shares=0):
        self.strategy = strategy
        self.cash = cash  # Money available to buy stocks
        self.shares = shares  # Shares owned

    def trade(self, market):
        """Decides whether to buy, sell, or hold based on strategy."""
        action = 0  # Default: Hold

        if self.strategy == "random":
            action = random.choice([-1, 0, 1])  # -1: Sell,
0: Hold, 1: Buy

        elif self.strategy == "trend_follower":
            if len(market.history) > 1 and market.history[-1]
> market.history[-2]:
                action = 1  # Buy when prices rise
            else:
                action = -1  # Sell when prices fall

        elif self.strategy == "value_investor":
            if market.price < np.mean(market.history[-5:]):
# Buy if price is low
                action = 1
            else:
                action = -1  # Sell if price is high

        # Execute trade
        if action == 1 and self.cash >= market.price:
            self.cash -= market.price
            self.shares += 1
            return 1  # Buy order
```

```python
        elif action == -1 and self.shares > 0:
            self.cash += market.price
            self.shares -= 1
            return -1  # Sell order
        return 0  # Hold

# Create traders
traders = [Trader(strategy=random.choice(["random",
"trend_follower", "value_investor"])) for _ in range(20)]
```

Each trader makes **independent buy/sell decisions** based on their strategy.

Step 3: Running the Market Simulation

Now, we run the simulation and see how stock prices evolve over time.

```python
python
----
# Initialize the market
market = Market()

# Run simulation for 50 time steps
for _ in range(50):
    trades = [trader.trade(market) for trader in traders]
    market.update_price(trades)

# Plot the stock price movement
market.plot_market()
```

What's Happening Here?

1. Each **trader** makes decisions based on their strategy.
2. The **market updates the stock price** based on the total buy/sell orders.
3. The **price fluctuates dynamically** over time, influenced by different trading styles.

The **price plot** will show real-time market dynamics—sometimes **trending up**, sometimes **crashing down**, depending on the **traders' collective behavior**.

Real-World Applications of MAS in Finance

- **Algorithmic Trading**
  High-frequency trading firms use **AI-driven MAS** to execute thousands of trades per second, responding to market conditions in milliseconds.
- **Market Crash Simulations**
  Financial institutions simulate market collapses by **modeling panic selling and investor sentiment**.
- **Central Bank Policy Testing**
  Governments simulate **interest rate changes and monetary policies** to predict economic effects before implementation.
- **Risk Management in Investment Portfolios**
  MAS-based models help hedge funds assess the **impact of global events on stock portfolios**.

Extending the Simulation

This basic model can be enhanced by:

- **Adding market shocks**: Simulating sudden crashes due to external events.
- **Introducing news sentiment analysis**: Traders reacting to news headlines.
- **Incorporating advanced AI agents**: Training Reinforcement Learning traders.
- **Expanding to multiple stocks**: Creating a **full financial ecosystem**.

MAS provides a **powerful lens** to understand financial markets, enabling researchers and professionals to model **real-world trading behavior**.

Our **simple market simulation** already shows how **traders influence price movement**. With more advanced AI techniques, MAS can **predict trends, prevent crashes, and even power the future of AI-driven investing**.

7.4 Multi-Agent Systems in Healthcare and Smart Cities

Multi-Agent Systems (MAS) are transforming **healthcare** and **smart cities** by enabling intelligent coordination, real-time decision-making, and adaptive responses to dynamic environments. From **automated patient monitoring** to **traffic optimization**, MAS helps build **smarter, more efficient systems** that improve lives.

In this chapter, we'll explore how MAS is applied in these domains and walk through a **hands-on simulation** of agent-based traffic management in a smart city.

Multi-Agent Systems in Healthcare

Healthcare is an inherently **complex, multi-agent environment** where doctors, nurses, patients, and even medical devices must interact efficiently. MAS helps in:

- **Hospital Resource Management**: Allocating hospital beds, scheduling surgeries, and managing medical staff.
- **Patient Monitoring & Emergency Response**: Smart wearable devices detecting health issues and notifying doctors in real-time.
- **Drug Discovery & Personalized Medicine**: AI agents analyzing genetic data to recommend targeted treatments.

Example: AI-Driven Patient Monitoring

Imagine a **hospital where AI agents monitor patients in real time**. A **MAS-based system** could consist of:

- **Sensor agents** collecting patient vitals.
- **Diagnosis agents** analyzing symptoms.
- **Alert agents** notifying doctors if a patient's condition worsens.

This setup reduces **response time** and ensures **efficient resource allocation**, improving patient outcomes.

Multi-Agent Systems in Smart Cities

Smart cities integrate **IoT sensors, AI, and MAS** to optimize urban life. MAS applications include:

- **Traffic management**: Reducing congestion with adaptive traffic signals.
- **Waste collection**: Coordinating garbage trucks efficiently.
- **Energy distribution**: Optimizing power grids based on demand.
- **Emergency response**: Directing ambulances along the fastest routes.

Building a Traffic Simulation for Smart Cities

Let's build a **MAS-based traffic simulation** where **traffic lights** and **vehicles** act as intelligent agents.

Step 1: Setting Up the Environment

First, install Mesa, a Python framework for agent-based modeling:

```bash
pip install mesa
```

Now, define a **traffic environment** where vehicles move and interact with smart traffic lights.

```python
from mesa import Agent, Model
from mesa.time import RandomActivation
from mesa.space import MultiGrid
import numpy as np
import matplotlib.pyplot as plt

class TrafficAgent(Agent):
    def __init__(self, unique_id, model):
        super().__init__(unique_id, model)
        self.speed = np.random.choice([1, 2])  # Randomized
vehicle speed

    def move(self):
        """Move vehicle forward if no obstruction."""
        x, y = self.pos
```

```python
            new_x = min(x + self.speed, self.model.grid.width -
1)
            if not any(isinstance(agent, TrafficLight) for agent
in self.model.grid.get_cell_list_contents((new_x, y))):
                self.model.grid.move_agent(self, (new_x, y))

    def step(self):
        """Execute one step in the simulation."""
        self.move()

class TrafficLight(Agent):
    def __init__(self, unique_id, model):
        super().__init__(unique_id, model)
        self.state = "green"
        self.timer = 0

    def step(self):
        """Switch traffic light state periodically."""
        self.timer += 1
        if self.timer % 5 == 0:
            self.state = "red" if self.state == "green" else
"green"
```

This creates:

- **TrafficAgent** (vehicles) that move unless blocked by a red light.
- **TrafficLight** (smart signals) that change every 5 steps.

Step 2: Building the Smart City Model

Now, define the **MAS model** and populate it with vehicles and traffic lights.

```python
----
class TrafficModel(Model):
    def __init__(self, width=10, height=1, num_vehicles=5):
        self.grid = MultiGrid(width, height, torus=False)
        self.schedule = RandomActivation(self)

        # Add vehicles
        for i in range(num_vehicles):
            vehicle = TrafficAgent(i, self)
            self.schedule.add(vehicle)
            self.grid.place_agent(vehicle, (i, 0))

        # Add a traffic light
        traffic_light = TrafficLight(num_vehicles, self)
```

```
        self.schedule.add(traffic_light)
        self.grid.place_agent(traffic_light, (width // 2, 0))

    def step(self):
        """Advance the model by one step."""
        self.schedule.step()
```

The **TrafficModel**:

- Initializes a **road** with a **grid layout**.
- Adds **vehicles** that move forward.
- Places **a smart traffic light** that controls flow.

Step 3: Running the Simulation

Now, let's **run the model** and visualize traffic movement.

```python
----
model = TrafficModel()
for _ in range(10):  # Run for 10 time steps
    model.step()

# Extract positions
vehicle_positions = [(agent.pos[0], i) for i, agent in
enumerate(model.schedule.agents) if isinstance(agent,
TrafficAgent)]

# Plot vehicle positions
plt.scatter(*zip(*vehicle_positions))
plt.xlabel("Road Position")
plt.ylabel("Vehicle ID")
plt.title("Traffic Simulation Snapshot")
plt.show()
```

This will display a **scatter plot** of vehicles' final positions, showing how traffic moves over time.

Real-World MAS Applications in Smart Cities

- **AI-Powered Traffic Control**
  Cities like **Singapore and Los Angeles** use **MAS-driven adaptive signals** to cut congestion.
- **Autonomous Vehicles Coordination**
  MAS helps **self-driving cars** communicate to **avoid collisions and optimize routes**.
- **Smart Energy Distribution**
  AI agents balance **electric grid loads** by **shifting power supply dynamically**.
- **Emergency Response Optimization**
  AI-driven systems **adjust traffic lights** for ambulances, reducing response times.

Extending the Simulation

This simple model can be expanded with:

- **Multiple intersections**: Simulating a full city grid.
- **Accident detection**: Vehicles slowing down for crashes.
- **Priority lanes**: Simulating buses and emergency vehicles.

Conclusion

Multi-Agent Systems are **revolutionizing healthcare and smart cities** by **coordinating complex interactions** in real-time.

From **intelligent hospitals** to **self-organizing urban traffic**, MAS **optimizes resource allocation, minimizes delays, and enhances decision-making**.

With further AI integration, MAS will **shape the future of intelligent, self-regulating cities and healthcare systems worldwide**.

Chapter 8: Testing, Debugging, and Optimization in Multi-Agent Systems

Developing a **Multi-Agent System (MAS)** is an exciting challenge, but the real test of its effectiveness comes when you **simulate, debug, and optimize** it. Without proper testing, agents may behave unpredictably, leading to inefficiencies, deadlocks, or even complete system failures.

In this chapter, we'll explore practical **testing methodologies, debugging strategies, and performance optimization techniques** for MAS. By the end, you'll be equipped with the skills to fine-tune your multi-agent simulations, ensuring **smooth, intelligent, and efficient agent interactions**.

8.1 Simulating and Testing Multi-Agent Scenarios

Imagine designing a **multi-agent system (MAS)** where autonomous drones collaborate to deliver packages. You've carefully programmed their behaviors, but when you test them, chaos unfolds—drones collide, deliveries get delayed, and some agents refuse to move. This is why **simulation and testing** are critical.

Multi-agent simulations help us **validate behaviors, identify issues, and fine-tune interactions** before deployment. Without testing, even the most sophisticated MAS could break down in real-world conditions.

In this section, we'll explore how to:

- **Set up a MAS simulation**
- **Run controlled experiments** to evaluate agent performance
- **Analyze and refine agent behaviors** based on test results

To make this hands-on, we'll use **Mesa**, a Python framework for multi-agent simulations.

Building a Multi-Agent Simulation

Let's simulate a **traffic intersection** managed by autonomous vehicles. Our goal is to test:

- Whether cars **avoid collisions**
- If traffic flows **efficiently**
- How different rules **impact congestion**

We'll create two types of agents:

1. **Car agents** that move in a specific direction
2. **Traffic light agents** that regulate movement

Step 1: Setting Up the Environment

We start by installing Mesa if you haven't already:

```bash
----
pip install mesa
```
Then, we create our simulation environment:
```python
----
from mesa import Agent, Model
from mesa.space import MultiGrid
from mesa.time import SimultaneousActivation

class TrafficModel(Model):
    def __init__(self, width, height, num_cars):
        self.grid = MultiGrid(width, height, torus=False)
        self.schedule = SimultaneousActivation(self)

        # Create traffic lights at intersections
        self.traffic_lights = [(3, 3), (6, 3), (3, 6), (6,
6)]
        for pos in self.traffic_lights:
            light = TrafficLightAgent(pos, self)
            self.grid.place_agent(light, pos)
            self.schedule.add(light)

        # Create car agents
        for i in range(num_cars):
            car = CarAgent(i, self)
            start_pos = (0, i % height)  # Staggered start
positions
            self.grid.place_agent(car, start_pos)
```

```
        self.schedule.add(car)

    def step(self):
        """Advance simulation by one step."""
        self.schedule.step()
```

This **TrafficModel**:

- Creates a **grid-based road system**
- Places **traffic lights at intersections**
- Spawns **car agents that move across the grid**

Step 2: Defining Agent Behaviors

Next, we define how cars and traffic lights behave.

Car Agent Behavior

Each **CarAgent** moves forward unless it encounters a red light.

```python
----
class CarAgent(Agent):
    def __init__(self, unique_id, model):
        super().__init__(unique_id, model)

    def step(self):
        """Move forward if the light ahead is green or if no
traffic light is present."""
        x, y = self.pos
        new_position = (x + 1, y)  # Move right

        # Check if there's a traffic light ahead
        ahead_agents =
self.model.grid.get_cell_list_contents(new_position)
        for agent in ahead_agents:
            if isinstance(agent, TrafficLightAgent) and not
agent.is_green:
                return  # Stop if light is red

        # Move to new position
        self.model.grid.move_agent(self, new_position)
```

Traffic Light Behavior

Traffic lights **switch between green and red** every few steps.

```python
class TrafficLightAgent(Agent):
    def __init__(self, pos, model):
        super().__init__(pos, model)
        self.is_green = True  # Start as green
        self.counter = 0

    def step(self):
        """Toggle light state every 5 steps."""
        self.counter += 1
        if self.counter % 5 == 0:
            self.is_green = not self.is_green
```

Step 3: Running and Visualizing the Simulation

To observe the system in action, we simulate it over multiple steps.

```python
model = TrafficModel(10, 10, num_cars=5)

for _ in range(20):  # Run 20 simulation steps
    model.step()
```

But how do we **see** what's happening? Let's add visualization.

```python
import matplotlib.pyplot as plt

def plot_traffic(model):
    """Visualize traffic simulation state."""
    car_positions = [agent.pos for agent in
model.schedule.agents if isinstance(agent, CarAgent)]
    light_positions = [agent.pos for agent in
model.schedule.agents if isinstance(agent,
TrafficLightAgent)]

    plt.figure(figsize=(6,6))
    plt.scatter(*zip(*car_positions), c='blue', label="Cars")
    plt.scatter(*zip(*light_positions), c='red',
label="Traffic Lights")
```

```
plt.xlim(0, model.grid.width)
plt.ylim(0, model.grid.height)
plt.grid()
plt.legend()
plt.title("Traffic Simulation State")
plt.show()

plot_traffic(model)
```

This plots:

- **Cars (blue dots)** moving through the grid
- **Traffic lights (red dots)** regulating intersections

With each step, we can **track congestion, stops, and movement patterns**.

Analyzing Simulation Results

To ensure the system works as expected, we monitor **key metrics**:

- **Average wait time** – Do cars spend too long at red lights?
- **Collision rate** – Do cars crash into each other?
- **Throughput** – How many cars successfully reach the end of the road?

We can collect and print these stats as follows:

```python
def collect_metrics(model):
    num_stopped = sum(1 for agent in model.schedule.agents if
isinstance(agent, CarAgent) and agent.pos in
model.traffic_lights)
    total_cars = sum(1 for agent in model.schedule.agents if
isinstance(agent, CarAgent))

    print(f"Stopped cars: {num_stopped} / {total_cars}")

for _ in range(20):
    model.step()
    collect_metrics(model)
```

Refining the System

Through simulation, we might discover:

Traffic jams – Cars bunch up at red lights.
Inefficient flow – Cars stop unnecessarily.
Deadlocks – No one moves due to bad light timing.

To **fix these issues**, we can:

- **Adjust traffic light timing** to balance green/red durations
- **Introduce adaptive traffic lights** that change based on congestion
- **Implement car priority rules** for smoother movement

For example, we can make **traffic lights adjust dynamically**:

```python
class SmartTrafficLightAgent(Agent):
    def step(self):
        """Turn green if too many cars are waiting."""
        num_waiting = sum(1 for agent in
self.model.grid.get_cell_list_contents(self.pos) if
isinstance(agent, CarAgent))
        self.is_green = num_waiting > 2  # Turn green if more
than 2 cars are waiting
```

This **optimizes flow dynamically**, preventing bottlenecks.

Testing and simulating MAS allows us to **spot inefficiencies, prevent failures, and optimize performance**. Key takeaways:

- **Simulating different traffic rules** helps refine decision-making.
- **Visualizing interactions** reveals inefficiencies.
- **Adjusting agent behaviors** improves flow and reduces congestion.

With these techniques, you can build **robust, intelligent multi-agent systems** that perform well in real-world scenarios.

8.2 Debugging Agent Interactions

Imagine running a multi-agent system (MAS) simulation where delivery drones navigate a city. Everything seems fine—until one drone starts circling endlessly, another crashes into a building, and a third completely ignores traffic rules. Debugging such unpredictable behaviors is one of the biggest challenges in MAS development.

When multiple agents interact, unexpected issues arise: miscommunications, deadlocks, unintended behaviors, and even agents working against each other. Debugging these systems requires structured techniques to **observe**, **analyze**, and **fix** problems efficiently.

In this section, we'll explore:

- Common issues in agent interactions
- Tools and strategies for debugging MAS
- A hands-on debugging workflow with Python and Mesa

Common Debugging Challenges in MAS

Before we dive into debugging methods, let's understand what typically goes wrong:

1. **Agents don't behave as expected** – They take incorrect actions, ignore signals, or make illogical decisions.
2. **Deadlocks occur** – Agents get stuck waiting for each other, leading to a standstill.
3. **Collisions and conflicts** – Agents interfere with each other, either physically (e.g., crashing into each other) or logically (e.g., competing for the same resource).
4. **Performance bottlenecks** – Simulations slow down due to inefficient agent logic.
5. **Non-deterministic behavior** – Runs produce different outcomes, making bugs hard to reproduce.

The key to fixing these issues is structured debugging—logging, visualization, and step-by-step analysis.

Debugging Strategies

1. Logging Agent Actions

The simplest yet most powerful tool in debugging is logging. By tracking what agents do at each step, we can identify unexpected behaviors.

Example: Adding Logs to an Agent Class

Let's consider a **robot agent** in a warehouse simulation. If the robots stop moving or behave unpredictably, logging can reveal the problem.

```python
import logging

# Set up logging
logging.basicConfig(level=logging.INFO, format='%(message)s')

class RobotAgent(Agent):
    def __init__(self, unique_id, model):
        super().__init__(unique_id, model)
        self.has_package = False  # Tracks if robot is carrying an item

    def step(self):
        if self.has_package:
            new_pos = (self.pos[0] + 1, self.pos[1])  # Move right
            logging.info(f"Agent {self.unique_id} moving to {new_pos} with package.")
        else:
            logging.info(f"Agent {self.unique_id} searching for a package.")
```

With logs, we can see each agent's movements, whether they pick up packages, and if they stop unexpectedly.

---

2. Using Breakpoints for Step-by-Step Debugging

For more complex bugs, inserting a **debugger breakpoint** helps analyze agent behavior step-by-step.

```python
import pdb  # Python debugger

class RobotAgent(Agent):
    def step(self):
        pdb.set_trace()  # Pauses execution and opens an
interactive debugger
        if self.has_package:
            new_pos = (self.pos[0] + 1, self.pos[1])
            self.model.grid.move_agent(self, new_pos)
```

When running the simulation, the **pdb** debugger will stop at this point, allowing us to inspect variables and agent states interactively.

---

3. Visualizing Agent Interactions

Debugging MAS is easier when we **see** how agents behave. We can use **Matplotlib** to visualize their movements and interactions.

Example: Plotting Agent Positions

```python
import matplotlib.pyplot as plt

def plot_agents(model):
    """Plots the positions of all agents in the
environment."""
    positions = [agent.pos for agent in
model.schedule.agents]

    plt.figure(figsize=(6, 6))
    plt.scatter(*zip(*positions), c='blue', label="Robots")
    plt.xlim(0, model.grid.width)
    plt.ylim(0, model.grid.height)
    plt.title("Robot Agent Positions")
    plt.legend()
    plt.grid()
    plt.show()

# Run the model and plot agent positions
for _ in range(10):
    model.step()

plot_agents(model)
```

This visualization quickly reveals patterns like congestion, stuck agents, or inefficient movement.

---

4. Detecting Deadlocks and Conflicts

Deadlocks happen when agents wait indefinitely due to conflicting actions.

Example: Detecting a Deadlock

```python
def detect_deadlock(model):
    """Checks if agents haven't moved for multiple steps."""
    static_agents = 0

    for agent in model.schedule.agents:
        if agent.pos == agent.prev_pos:
            static_agents += 1
        agent.prev_pos = agent.pos  # Update previous
position

    if static_agents == len(model.schedule.agents):
        print("Potential deadlock detected! Agents are
stuck.")

# Run model and check for deadlocks
for _ in range(10):
    model.step()
    detect_deadlock(model)
```

If **all agents remain in the same position**, we likely have a deadlock. We can then investigate why and adjust agent decision rules.

---

5. Analyzing Performance Issues

If a MAS simulation runs too slowly, profiling can identify performance bottlenecks.

Example: Profiling Execution Time

```
python
----
import time

start_time = time.time()

# Run simulation
for _ in range(100):
    model.step()

end_time = time.time()
print(f"Simulation time: {end_time - start_time:.2f}
seconds")
```

If execution takes too long, possible optimizations include:

- **Reducing agent decision complexity**
- **Using vectorized operations** instead of loops
- **Parallelizing computations** with multiprocessing

Case Study: Debugging a Multi-Agent Traffic Simulation

Let's debug an issue in our earlier **traffic simulation** where cars **collide at intersections**.

Step 1: Identifying the Problem

We notice that:

1. Some cars **ignore red lights**.
2. Cars **occupy the same space**, causing collisions.

Step 2: Adding Debugging Tools

We log each car's movement and use visualization to spot issues.

```
python
----
for _ in range(10):
    model.step()
    plot_traffic(model)    # Plots each simulation step
    collect_metrics(model)  # Logs stopped cars
```

Step 3: Finding the Root Cause

By analyzing logs, we discover that:

- The **traffic light rule wasn't consistently applied**
- Some cars **moved into occupied spaces**

Step 4: Fixing the Issues

We refine the agent logic:

```python
class CarAgent(Agent):
    def step(self):
        x, y = self.pos
        new_position = (x + 1, y)

        # Prevent movement into occupied spaces
        if self.model.grid.is_cell_empty(new_position):
            self.model.grid.move_agent(self, new_position)
```

We also **strictly enforce traffic light rules**.

```python
if isinstance(agent_ahead, TrafficLightAgent) and not
agent_ahead.is_green:
    return  # Stop at red light
```

Step 5: Re-Testing and Validating Fixes

After making changes, we **rerun the simulation** and **check logs and visualizations**. If collisions no longer occur, the fix is successful.

Debugging multi-agent interactions requires a **systematic approach**:

1. **Observe behaviors with logging and visualization.**
2. **Use breakpoints for step-by-step debugging.**
3. **Detect deadlocks and performance issues proactively.**
4. **Validate fixes through multiple test runs.**

By combining these techniques, you can refine your MAS and **ensure smooth, intelligent agent interactions**.

8.3 Performance Optimization Techniques

Imagine running a **multi-agent system (MAS) simulation** with hundreds of agents—robots in a warehouse, traffic on a smart grid, or AI traders in a stock market. Initially, everything runs smoothly. But as the number of agents increases, the system slows to a crawl. Simulations take forever, agent responses lag, and memory consumption skyrockets.

Performance bottlenecks are a common challenge in MAS, but they can be tackled with the right techniques. In this section, we'll cover practical ways to optimize your MAS, from improving agent logic to leveraging parallel computing. We'll also walk through hands-on examples so you can apply these techniques in your own projects.

Why Performance Optimization Matters

A well-optimized MAS is not just about speed—it's about **scalability**. The ability to efficiently handle increasing agent numbers is crucial for real-world applications. Poor performance can lead to:

- **Slow decision-making** in critical systems (e.g., autonomous vehicles)
- **Inaccurate simulations** due to missing interactions (e.g., real-time market models)
- **High computational costs** for large-scale simulations

By fine-tuning the system, we ensure agents interact in real-time, making intelligent decisions without unnecessary delays.

Key Optimization Strategies

1. Optimize Agent Decision Logic

One of the biggest performance killers is inefficient agent logic. If each agent performs unnecessary calculations or redundant checks, execution slows dramatically.

Example: Simplifying Decision Logic

Consider a **robot delivery system**, where each agent calculates its path at every step. Instead of recalculating paths needlessly, we **cache** previous routes when the environment hasn't changed.

```python
class RobotAgent(Agent):
    def __init__(self, unique_id, model):
        super().__init__(unique_id, model)
        self.cached_path = None  # Store the last computed path

    def step(self):
        if self.cached_path and not self.model.grid.has_obstacle(self.cached_path):
            # Use cached path if still valid
            self.move_along(self.cached_path)
        else:
            # Compute a new path only when necessary
            self.cached_path = self.compute_new_path()
            self.move_along(self.cached_path)
```

By reducing unnecessary recalculations, the system runs **significantly faster** without sacrificing accuracy.

---

2. Reduce Redundant Agent Interactions

Many MAS simulations require agents to check their surroundings, but doing so **inefficiently** slows performance. Instead of scanning the entire grid, use **spatial partitioning** to check only relevant neighbors.

Example: Efficient Neighbor Search

```python
def get_nearby_agents(self):
    """Fetch agents in a smaller radius instead of scanning the entire grid."""
```

```
    return self.model.grid.get_neighbors(self.pos, radius=2,
include_center=False)
```

By limiting the search radius, each agent interacts with only nearby entities, making the system **more efficient**.

---

3. Use Vectorized Operations Instead of Loops

In Python, loops over large datasets slow down performance. Instead, we can use **NumPy** for optimized calculations.

Example: Vectorized Computation for Traffic Flow

Instead of looping through each vehicle to compute speed adjustments, we can use **NumPy arrays** for faster calculations.

```python
----
import numpy as np

# Example speed update for all cars
speeds = np.array([car.speed for car in cars])
accelerations = np.array([car.acceleration for car in cars])

new_speeds = speeds + accelerations  # Vectorized operation
```

This approach can be **10x faster** than a traditional loop.

---

4. Parallelizing Agent Execution

If agent decisions are independent, they can be **executed in parallel** using multiprocessing.

Example: Running Agents in Parallel

```python
----
from multiprocessing import Pool

def agent_step(agent):
    agent.step()
```

```
with Pool() as pool:
    pool.map(agent_step, model.schedule.agents)
```

By distributing agent execution across multiple CPU cores, performance improves dramatically for large-scale MAS simulations.

5. Leveraging Efficient Data Structures

Using the right data structures can drastically reduce execution time.

- **Use dictionaries for quick lookups** instead of lists.
- **Use sets for membership checks** instead of iterating through a list.
- **Store agent states in NumPy arrays** instead of native Python lists.

Example: Using a Dictionary for Fast Access

```python
# Instead of searching a list, use a dictionary
agent_positions = {agent.unique_id: agent.pos for agent in
model.schedule.agents}

# Quick lookup
pos = agent_positions.get(target_agent_id)
```

This avoids slow linear searches, improving execution speed.

6. Profiling and Identifying Bottlenecks

Before optimizing, it's crucial to **identify where the bottlenecks are**. Using Python's **cProfile** helps pinpoint slow parts of the code.

Example: Profiling a MAS Simulation

```python
import cProfile

cProfile.run('model.run(100)')
```

This generates a report showing which functions consume the most time. Once identified, we focus optimization efforts where they matter most.

Case Study: Optimizing a Smart City Traffic Simulation

Let's say we have a **traffic simulation** with 1,000 cars navigating a city grid. Initially, performance is slow due to:

- **Inefficient routing calculations** – Cars recalculate paths at every step.
- **Excessive agent interactions** – Each car scans all others for collisions.
- **Loop-based data processing** – Speed adjustments are done in loops.

Step 1: Caching Route Calculations

Instead of recalculating routes every step, we **store and reuse** previous routes.

```python
class CarAgent(Agent):
    def __init__(self, unique_id, model):
        super().__init__(unique_id, model)
        self.cached_route = None

    def step(self):
        if not self.cached_route:
            self.cached_route = self.compute_route()
        self.follow_route(self.cached_route)
```

Step 2: Limiting Neighbor Searches

Instead of scanning all cars, we **check only nearby cars** using spatial partitioning.

```python
def get_nearby_cars(self):
    """Only checks cars within a small radius."""
    return self.model.grid.get_neighbors(self.pos, radius=3,
include_center=False)
```

Step 3: Using Vectorized Speed Calculations

```python
import numpy as np

car_speeds = np.array([car.speed for car in
model.schedule.agents])
car_speeds += np.array([car.acceleration for car in
model.schedule.agents])
```

With these optimizations, **simulation time drops from 10 minutes to under a minute**.

Final Thoughts

Optimizing MAS performance isn't just about making things run faster—it's about **scaling** efficiently. By **streamlining agent logic, reducing redundant computations, leveraging vectorization, and using parallel execution**, we can build MAS simulations that handle thousands (or even millions) of agents efficiently.

When working on performance improvements, remember:

- **Profile first** – Identify where the real bottlenecks are.
- **Simplify agent logic** – Avoid unnecessary calculations.
- **Use optimized data structures** – Prefer dictionaries, sets, and NumPy arrays.
- **Leverage parallelism** – Take advantage of multiprocessing when possible.

By applying these techniques, you can build MAS simulations that are **fast, scalable, and ready for real-world applications**.

Chapter 9: Deploying Multi-Agent Systems

Building a multi-agent system (MAS) is one thing—deploying it at scale is another challenge entirely. Whether you're running **thousands of autonomous drones**, **millions of financial trading bots**, or **a network of smart city sensors**, ensuring that agents communicate efficiently and make decisions in real-time is critical.

In this chapter, we'll explore practical strategies for **scaling MAS**, deploying them using **cloud and distributed computing**, and integrating them with **AI and IoT systems**. You'll get hands-on guidance and examples that will help you bring your MAS to production efficiently.

9.1 Scaling MAS for Large-Scale Applications

Multi-Agent Systems (MAS) can start small—a handful of agents working together on a simple problem. But what happens when you need to scale? Whether you're building **thousands of trading bots**, **a swarm of delivery drones**, or **a distributed AI assistant network**, scaling MAS introduces new challenges.

In this chapter, we'll explore **why scaling matters**, the main bottlenecks that arise, and **practical techniques** to ensure that your MAS remains **efficient, responsive, and scalable**. You'll also get hands-on implementations, so you can see these strategies in action.

Why Scaling Matters

Scaling isn't just about adding more agents. As the number of agents grows, new problems emerge:

- **Computational load increases** – More agents mean more decisions, requiring smarter resource management.
- **Communication overload** – If every agent talks to every other agent, the system can become **too slow** to function properly.
- **Coordination complexity** – More agents interacting means a higher chance of conflicts, redundant work, or inefficiencies.

A well-designed MAS should **scale efficiently**, ensuring that adding more agents improves performance instead of making things worse.

Key Strategies for Scaling MAS

1. Distributed Execution: Spreading the Workload

If all agents are running on a single system, performance will hit a bottleneck. One solution is to **distribute** the workload across multiple machines.

A **parallel computing framework** like **Ray** helps scale MAS by spreading computation across multiple CPUs or even different machines.

Example: Running Thousands of Agents in Parallel with Ray

```python
import ray

ray.init()  # Initialize Ray

@ray.remote
class Agent:
    def __init__(self, agent_id):
        self.agent_id = agent_id

    def step(self):
        return f"Agent {self.agent_id} executed a step."

# Create 1000 agents, each running in parallel
agents = [Agent.remote(i) for i in range(1000)]

# Run agent steps concurrently
results = ray.get([agent.step.remote() for agent in agents])

print(results[:5])  # Display a few results
```

Here's what's happening:

- **Each agent runs independently**, without blocking others.
- **Ray distributes workload across available CPUs/machines**, making execution **much faster** than running everything sequentially.
- **Scales to thousands of agents**, even across multiple machines.

2. Hierarchical Agent Structures: Reducing Communication Bottlenecks

If every agent tries to communicate with every other agent, network traffic explodes. Instead of a **fully connected** MAS, a **hierarchical model** helps **reduce communication overload**.

Think of it like a **military chain of command**:

- **Low-level agents** handle local decisions.
- **Mid-level agents** summarize and relay information.
- **High-level agents** make strategic decisions.

This reduces unnecessary communication and **keeps MAS responsive at scale**.

Example: Implementing a Hierarchical MAS

```python
----
class LowLevelAgent:
    def __init__(self, agent_id):
        self.agent_id = agent_id

    def perform_task(self):
        return f"Agent {self.agent_id} completed a task."

class MidLevelAgent:
    def __init__(self, group_id, agents):
        self.group_id = group_id
        self.agents = agents

    def summarize_tasks(self):
        results = [agent.perform_task() for agent in
self.agents]
        return f"Group {self.group_id} summary:
{len(results)} tasks completed."

# Create low-level agents
low_level_agents = [LowLevelAgent(i) for i in range(10)]

# Create a mid-level agent managing them
mid_level = MidLevelAgent(group_id=1,
agents=low_level_agents)
```

```
print(mid_level.summarize_tasks())
```

With this structure:

- **Only mid-level agents communicate with higher levels**, reducing message overload.
- **The system stays organized**, even with thousands of agents.
- **Scaling up is easier**—just add more mid-level layers as needed.

---

3. Cloud Deployment for Infinite Scalability

When a MAS gets too large for a single system, **cloud computing** is the answer. Deploying agents in the cloud allows **on-demand scaling**, running only as many resources as needed.

Example: Deploying MAS Agents on Kubernetes

Kubernetes lets us **deploy MAS as microservices**, so each agent runs **independently**, scaling as needed.

1. **Create a Docker container for an agent:**

```dockerfile
# Dockerfile
FROM python:3.9
WORKDIR /app
COPY agent.py .
CMD ["python", "agent.py"]
```

2. **Define a Kubernetes deployment:**

```yaml
apiVersion: apps/v1
kind: Deployment
metadata:
  name: mas-agent
spec:
  replicas: 50  # Deploy 50 agents
  selector:
    matchLabels:
      app: mas-agent
  template:
```

```
metadata:
  labels:
    app: mas-agent
spec:
  containers:
  - name: mas-agent
    image: mas-agent:latest
```

3. **Deploy to Kubernetes:**

```sh
kubectl apply -f agent-deployment.yaml
```

Now we have **50 MAS agents running in the cloud**, and we can **scale up dynamically**.

---

4. Optimizing Communication: Using Message Brokers

Instead of **every agent sending messages to every other agent**, a **message broker** like **RabbitMQ** or **Kafka** can **efficiently route** communication.

Example: MAS Communication with RabbitMQ

```python
import pika

connection =
pika.BlockingConnection(pika.ConnectionParameters('localhost'
))
channel = connection.channel()
channel.queue_declare(queue='task_queue')

# Sending a message
channel.basic_publish(exchange='', routing_key='task_queue',
body='Agent task data')
print(" [x] Sent 'Agent task data'")
connection.close()
```

With a message broker:

- Agents **only receive relevant messages** instead of being bombarded with data.
- Communication **remains efficient**, even with **millions of agents**.

Scaling MAS **isn't just about adding more agents**—it's about designing systems that remain efficient at larger scales.

Key Takeaways:

- **Use parallel computing** (e.g., Ray) to distribute computation efficiently.
- **Structure agents hierarchically** to reduce communication overload.
- **Deploy MAS in the cloud** for scalability and flexibility.
- **Use message brokers** to streamline agent communication.

With these strategies, your MAS will be ready to **scale from a few agents to thousands—or even millions—without breaking down.**

9.2 Cloud and Distributed Computing for Multi-Agent Systems

When building a **Multi-Agent System (MAS)**, a single machine can only take you so far. Once your agents start handling complex tasks, coordinating large-scale simulations, or processing real-time data streams, **you'll need more computing power**. That's where **cloud computing and distributed systems** come in.

In this chapter, we'll dive into **why the cloud is essential for MAS**, how to deploy your agents across multiple servers, and **practical implementations using cloud platforms**. We'll also explore **message passing, scalability, and fault tolerance**—critical components for ensuring a MAS remains efficient and reliable.

Why Cloud and Distributed Computing Matter for MAS

Imagine you're running **thousands of autonomous delivery drones** or **a global stock-trading bot network**. If all agents rely on a single system, **you'll hit performance bottlenecks fast**.

By **distributing agents across multiple cloud servers**, you can:

- Scale **infinitely** as demand grows.
- Ensure **fault tolerance**—if one server fails, the system keeps running.
- Process **huge datasets** efficiently by parallelizing computations.

Cloud computing offers a flexible and cost-effective way to **deploy, manage, and scale** a MAS.

Deploying MAS in the Cloud

To run agents in a cloud environment, we need:

- A **distributed framework** to manage agent execution.
- A **message-passing system** for inter-agent communication.
- A **scalable architecture** that adapts to workload changes.

Let's walk through **how to deploy MAS in the cloud using Kubernetes and Ray**.

---

1. Running a Multi-Agent System on Kubernetes

Kubernetes is a **container orchestration platform** that helps deploy MAS in the cloud. Each agent runs inside a **container**, and Kubernetes manages **scaling, networking, and fault recovery**.

Step 1: Containerizing an MAS Agent

First, we **package our agent code** into a Docker container.

Agent Code (agent.py)

```python
----
import time

def run_agent(agent_id):
    while True:
```

```
        print(f"Agent {agent_id} processing data...")
        time.sleep(5)

if __name__ == "__main__":
    import sys
    run_agent(sys.argv[1])
```

Dockerfile

```dockerfile
FROM python:3.9
WORKDIR /app
COPY agent.py .
CMD ["python", "agent.py", "1"]
```

Build and test the container:

```sh
docker build -t mas-agent .
docker run mas-agent
```

Now that we have a working agent, let's deploy it to **Kubernetes**.

Step 2: Deploying MAS Agents in Kubernetes

We define a **Kubernetes Deployment** to run multiple agent instances.

Deployment File (agent-deployment.yaml)

```yaml
apiVersion: apps/v1
kind: Deployment
metadata:
  name: mas-agent
spec:
  replicas: 10   # Deploy 10 agents
  selector:
    matchLabels:
      app: mas-agent
  template:
    metadata:
      labels:
        app: mas-agent
```

```
spec:
  containers:
  - name: mas-agent
    image: mas-agent:latest
```

Deploy to **Kubernetes**:

```sh
kubectl apply -f agent-deployment.yaml
```

Now we have **10 agent instances running in parallel** in the cloud!

---

2. Distributed Computing with Ray

For MAS workloads that require **parallel computation** (e.g., reinforcement learning, data processing), **Ray** is an excellent framework.

With **Ray**, we can run MAS agents across multiple cloud machines with minimal setup.

Step 1: Installing Ray

First, install Ray:

```sh
pip install ray
```

Step 2: Running MAS Agents on a Distributed Cluster

We define a **multi-agent execution model** using Ray's remote execution.

```python
import ray

ray.init()  # Initialize Ray cluster

@ray.remote
class MASAgent:
    def __init__(self, agent_id):
        self.agent_id = agent_id
```

```
    def compute_task(self):
        return f"Agent {self.agent_id} completed a task."

# Create multiple agents
agents = [MASAgent.remote(i) for i in range(100)]

# Execute tasks in parallel
results = ray.get([agent.compute_task.remote() for agent in
agents])

print(results[:5])  # Display sample results
```

Why Use Ray for MAS?

- **Automatically scales** across cloud machines.
- **Efficient parallel execution** for thousands of agents.
- **Easy integration** with cloud platforms (AWS, GCP, Azure).

If your MAS needs **high-speed computation**, Ray is a game-changer.

---

3. Scalable Agent Communication with Message Queues

In large-scale MAS, agents need to communicate **without overwhelming the network**. A **message broker** like **RabbitMQ or Kafka** helps **manage and distribute messages efficiently**.

Step 1: Setting Up RabbitMQ for Agent Communication

First, install **RabbitMQ** and the required library:

```sh
----
pip install pika
```

Step 2: Sending Messages Between Agents

Producer (Agent Sending a Task Message)

```python
----
import pika
```

```
connection =
pika.BlockingConnection(pika.ConnectionParameters('localhost'
))
channel = connection.channel()
channel.queue_declare(queue='tasks')

channel.basic_publish(exchange='', routing_key='tasks',
body='Task assigned')
print(" [x] Task message sent")

connection.close()
```

Consumer (Agent Receiving the Task Message)

```python
----
import pika

def callback(ch, method, properties, body):
    print(f" [x] Received task: {body.decode()}")

connection =
pika.BlockingConnection(pika.ConnectionParameters('localhost'
))
channel = connection.channel()
channel.queue_declare(queue='tasks')

channel.basic_consume(queue='tasks',
on_message_callback=callback, auto_ack=True)
print(' [*] Waiting for messages...')
channel.start_consuming()
```

With **message queues**, MAS can:

- Efficiently **route tasks** between agents.
- Avoid **communication bottlenecks**.
- Ensure **agents only receive relevant data**.

Scaling MAS in the cloud is about **efficiency, resilience, and cost-effectiveness**.

Key Takeaways:

- Use **Kubernetes** to deploy and scale MAS agents in the cloud.
- Leverage **Ray** for high-speed, distributed agent execution.

- Implement **message queues** for scalable agent communication.

By combining **cloud computing, distributed execution, and efficient messaging**, your MAS can handle **millions of agents, complex environments, and real-time decision-making at scale**.

9.3 Integrating Multi-Agent Systems with AI and IoT Systems

The real power of **Multi-Agent Systems (MAS)** is unlocked when they are combined with **Artificial Intelligence (AI) and the Internet of Things (IoT)**. Imagine a fleet of **autonomous drones** coordinating to deliver packages, a network of **smart sensors** optimizing energy use in a city, or AI-powered **financial bots** dynamically adjusting trading strategies based on real-time data. These are all examples of MAS integrating with AI and IoT.

In this chapter, we'll explore **how MAS can work seamlessly with AI for decision-making** and how **IoT devices can provide real-world data** to enhance agent interactions. We'll also walk through **a practical implementation** where MAS agents use IoT sensors and AI models to make intelligent decisions.

Why Integrate MAS with AI and IoT?

When we bring **AI and IoT** into MAS, we create **intelligent, data-driven, real-world applications**.

- **AI helps agents make smarter decisions** by predicting trends, recognizing patterns, and optimizing outcomes.
- **IoT connects agents to the physical world**, providing **real-time environmental data** that agents can act upon.

Consider a **smart warehouse**: AI-powered MAS agents **control robots**, IoT sensors **track inventory**, and **AI algorithms optimize logistics**. The result? **Efficient operations, reduced costs, and faster deliveries**.

Building an AI + IoT-Powered MAS

Let's build a **smart energy management system** where:

- **MAS agents** manage energy distribution.
- **IoT sensors** collect real-time data (temperature, power usage).
- **AI models** predict energy demand and optimize consumption.

Step 1: Setting Up IoT Sensors

First, we simulate an IoT environment where sensors send **temperature and energy usage data** to MAS agents.

Simulating IoT Data with MQTT

MQTT (Message Queuing Telemetry Transport) is a lightweight protocol used for IoT communication. We'll use the **paho-mqtt** library to send sensor data.

Install it using:

```sh
pip install paho-mqtt
```

Create an **IoT sensor simulator** that sends real-time data.

```python
import paho.mqtt.client as mqtt
import random
import time

BROKER = "broker.hivemq.com"
TOPIC = "smartcity/energy"

client = mqtt.Client()
client.connect(BROKER, 1883, 60)

while True:
    temperature = round(random.uniform(18, 35), 2)   #
Simulated temperature
    power_usage = round(random.uniform(100, 500), 2)  # Power
in watts
```

```
data = f"{temperature},{power_usage}"

client.publish(TOPIC, data)
print(f"Sent data: {data}")

time.sleep(5)  # Send data every 5 seconds
```

This script **mimics an IoT sensor** by sending temperature and power usage data every **5 seconds** to an MQTT broker.

Step 2: Creating MAS Agents to Process IoT Data

Now, let's define **MAS agents** that listen to IoT data and optimize energy distribution.

Agent Code (energy_agent.py)

```python
----
import paho.mqtt.client as mqtt
import time

BROKER = "broker.hivemq.com"
TOPIC = "smartcity/energy"

def on_message(client, userdata, msg):
    temperature, power_usage = map(float,
msg.payload.decode().split(","))

    # Simple AI-based decision-making
    if temperature > 30 and power_usage > 400:
        decision = "Reduce power consumption"
    else:
        decision = "Normal operation"

    print(f"Received -> Temp: {temperature}°C, Power:
{power_usage}W | Decision: {decision}")

client = mqtt.Client()
client.on_message = on_message
client.connect(BROKER, 1883, 60)
client.subscribe(TOPIC)

print("Agent listening for IoT data...")
client.loop_forever()
```

How This Works:

- The agent **subscribes** to the IoT topic.
- It **receives sensor data** and makes decisions based on AI logic.
- If **high power usage and high temperature** are detected, it **reduces power consumption**.

Step 3: Enhancing Decision-Making with AI

To improve decision-making, we integrate **machine learning**. Instead of **if-else rules**, we'll train an **AI model** to predict **optimal power usage** based on sensor data.

Training an AI Model

```python
import pandas as pd
import numpy as np
from sklearn.ensemble import RandomForestRegressor
from sklearn.model_selection import train_test_split

# Simulated IoT dataset
data = {
    "temperature": np.random.uniform(18, 35, 500),
    "power_usage": np.random.uniform(100, 500, 500),
}
df = pd.DataFrame(data)
df["optimal_power"] = df["power_usage"] * (1 -
(df["temperature"] / 100))  # Artificial formula

X = df[["temperature", "power_usage"]]
y = df["optimal_power"]

X_train, X_test, y_train, y_test = train_test_split(X, y,
test_size=0.2, random_state=42)

model = RandomForestRegressor(n_estimators=100)
model.fit(X_train, y_train)

print("AI Model Trained!")
```

Using the AI Model in MAS Agents

Now, instead of simple rules, our MAS agents **predict optimal power usage** dynamically.

```python
----
import pickle
import paho.mqtt.client as mqtt
import numpy as np

# Load trained AI model
model = pickle.load(open("energy_model.pkl", "rb"))

BROKER = "broker.hivemq.com"
TOPIC = "smartcity/energy"

def on_message(client, userdata, msg):
    temperature, power_usage = map(float,
msg.payload.decode().split(","))

    # AI-based prediction
    optimal_power = model.predict(np.array([[temperature,
power_usage]]))[0]

    print(f"Received -> Temp: {temperature}°C, Power:
{power_usage}W | Predicted Optimal Power: {optimal_power}W")

client = mqtt.Client()
client.on_message = on_message
client.connect(BROKER, 1883, 60)
client.subscribe(TOPIC)

print("Agent listening for IoT data...")
client.loop_forever()
```

Now, instead of **static rules**, our MAS agents **learn from real-world patterns** and **adjust dynamically**.

Final Thoughts

Integrating **MAS with AI and IoT** enables **real-world intelligence, automation, and adaptability**.

Key Takeaways:

- **IoT sensors provide real-time data** to MAS agents.
- **AI enhances decision-making** by predicting optimal actions.
- **Cloud-based MAS** ensures scalability and fault tolerance.

From **smart cities** to **autonomous vehicles**, MAS + AI + IoT is shaping the future.

Chapter 10: Future Trends and Ethical Considerations in Multi-Agent Systems

As multi-agent systems (MAS) continue to evolve, their impact on **AI-driven automation, decision-making, and real-world applications** is growing rapidly. From **autonomous vehicles coordinating on highways** to **intelligent trading bots in financial markets**, MAS is at the heart of next-generation AI solutions.

In this final chapter, we explore **cutting-edge research, ethical concerns, and the road ahead** for MAS. By the end, you'll have a **clear understanding of the opportunities and challenges** that will shape the future of MAS.

10.1 Advances in MAS Research

Multi-agent systems (MAS) are rapidly transforming the landscape of **artificial intelligence, automation, and large-scale decision-making**. From coordinating self-driving cars to optimizing global supply chains, the capabilities of MAS are advancing at an unprecedented pace. These systems are no longer limited to theoretical models; they are now **solving real-world problems** with increasing autonomy and intelligence.

In this chapter, we explore the most **cutting-edge developments in MAS research**, focusing on **learning-based approaches, decentralized architectures, and large-scale simulations**. By the end, you'll have a clear picture of where MAS is headed and how these advancements are shaping the future of AI-driven decision-making.

Learning-Based Multi-Agent Systems

Traditional MAS relied on **rule-based strategies and game theory**, where agents followed predefined instructions to interact with their environment. However, as real-world problems become more complex, researchers have turned to **learning-based approaches** that allow agents to **adapt, collaborate, and evolve** over time.

Multi-Agent Reinforcement Learning (MARL)

One of the biggest breakthroughs in MAS is the integration of **reinforcement learning (RL)**. Instead of relying on static rules, agents use **trial and error** to discover optimal strategies for collaboration or competition.

For example, in **multi-agent traffic control**, reinforcement learning enables smart traffic lights to **adjust in real-time** based on congestion patterns, significantly reducing delays. Google's AI-driven traffic optimization has already demonstrated **up to a 25% improvement in traffic flow** in cities where it's deployed.

In gaming, MARL was famously used by **OpenAI Five**, a team of AI agents that **outperformed human world champions in Dota 2** by learning advanced teamwork strategies. These AI-driven teams were not pre-programmed with tactics; instead, they learned through millions of simulated matches, refining their ability to **anticipate opponents and cooperate with teammates**.

Decentralized and Distributed MAS

Most traditional AI systems rely on centralized computing, where decisions are processed in a single location (like a cloud server). However, many modern MAS applications require **real-time, decentralized decision-making**.

Edge Computing and Federated Learning

Decentralized MAS leverages **edge computing**, where agents process data **locally** rather than sending it to the cloud. This is crucial for applications like **self-driving cars, drone fleets, and IoT networks**, where **latency and privacy** are major concerns.

A major innovation in this area is **federated learning**, which allows agents to **train AI models locally** and share updates without exposing sensitive data. This approach is already being used in **healthcare**, where hospitals collaborate on AI-powered diagnostics while maintaining patient confidentiality.

In financial markets, **decentralized MAS trading algorithms** are reshaping how transactions are executed. AI-powered trading agents now operate **autonomously across multiple exchanges**, identifying arbitrage opportunities and executing trades in milliseconds—all while adapting to market fluctuations.

MAS in Large-Scale Simulations

As AI advances, MAS is playing a crucial role in **simulating and predicting complex systems**. Researchers now use MAS to **model climate change, disaster response, and urban development** with unprecedented accuracy.

Digital Twins and Smart Cities

A fascinating real-world application of MAS is **digital twin technology**, where cities create **virtual copies of real-world infrastructure** to test new policies before implementing them.

For example, Singapore has developed an AI-driven digital twin of the entire city, allowing officials to **simulate traffic scenarios, energy consumption, and emergency responses**. Before modifying traffic light sequences, urban planners can first test their impact in the digital environment—saving both time and money while avoiding unnecessary disruptions.

The Future of MAS Research

MAS is evolving rapidly, but its future depends on **solving key challenges** such as bias in AI, security risks, and ethical concerns in autonomous decision-making. The next frontier will likely involve **combining MAS with advances in quantum computing and neuro-symbolic AI**, creating systems that can think, reason, and collaborate more effectively than ever before.

With these breakthroughs, MAS is set to **redefine how machines interact, learn, and make decisions**, paving the way for **more intelligent, scalable, and autonomous AI systems**.

10.2 Ethical and Security Challenges in Multi-Agent Systems

Multi-agent systems (MAS) are becoming a powerful force in **autonomous decision-making, real-time coordination, and large-scale automation**. But as MAS take on greater roles in **finance, healthcare, military applications, and critical infrastructure**, their ethical and security risks grow.

What happens when **AI-driven stock traders manipulate financial markets**? How do we ensure that **self-driving cars make fair decisions** in unavoidable accidents? And how do we **prevent malicious agents from disrupting systems** designed to improve society?

This chapter explores the **ethical dilemmas and security risks of MAS**, along with strategies to address them.

Ethical Challenges in Multi-Agent Systems

As MAS gain autonomy, they make decisions that **affect humans directly**. The core ethical challenges revolve around **fairness, accountability, transparency, and bias**.

Bias and Fairness in Agent Decision-Making

MAS, like all AI systems, learn from **data**. If this data is **biased**, the agents can **unintentionally reinforce discrimination**.

Consider AI-powered hiring systems used by corporations. If a hiring MAS is trained on **historical employment data where certain demographics were underrepresented**, it may automatically **reject qualified candidates** from those backgrounds.

Similarly, **autonomous loan approval agents** have been shown to **deny loans unfairly** to marginalized communities due to biased training data.

Solving this issue requires:

- **Careful data curation** to ensure diversity.

- **Regular audits** to detect and correct bias.
- **Fairness constraints** in AI models to prevent discrimination.

Accountability and the "Black Box" Problem

A major challenge with MAS is that their decision-making processes can be **hard to understand**, especially with deep learning-based agents.

For example, if a **self-driving taxi causes an accident**, who is responsible? The software engineers, the car manufacturer, or the AI system itself?

MAS should be designed with:

- **Explainability**: Agents should provide a **clear rationale** for decisions.
- **Human-in-the-loop oversight**: Critical decisions should involve **human review** before execution.

Moral Decision-Making in Autonomous Agents

What if a self-driving ambulance must choose between **hitting a pedestrian or crashing into another vehicle**? How should an **AI military drone** decide whether to **engage a target**?

Moral decision-making in MAS is complex. Some proposed solutions include:

- **Encoding ethical frameworks** into agent behavior.
- **Using collective human input** to train MAS on acceptable moral choices.
- **Restricting AI autonomy** in scenarios with high ethical risks.

Security Risks in Multi-Agent Systems

MAS operate in **dynamic environments** and interact with **other agents, humans, and digital systems**. This makes them vulnerable to various security threats, including hacking, adversarial attacks, and manipulation.

Adversarial Attacks on MAS

MAS rely on machine learning models, which are **susceptible to adversarial attacks**—where an attacker subtly manipulates inputs to trick an agent.

For example, researchers have shown that **small stickers placed on road signs** can **confuse self-driving cars**, making them misinterpret a stop sign as a speed limit sign.

Similarly, **malicious trading bots** in stock markets can create **false demand signals**, tricking other AI agents into making poor investment decisions.

To counter these threats, MAS developers must:

- **Use robust adversarial training** to detect manipulation.
- **Implement anomaly detection systems** to identify suspicious agent behavior.
- **Regularly test agents against evolving attack strategies**.

MAS in Cyber Warfare and Misinformation

MAS are increasingly used in cybersecurity, but they are also **weapons in cyber warfare**. Autonomous agents can:

- **Launch coordinated cyberattacks** against financial institutions or national infrastructure.
- **Spread misinformation online** through bot networks, influencing elections or public opinion.

Addressing these risks requires:

- **Stronger authentication protocols** for AI-driven agents.
- **Better monitoring of online agent behavior** to detect misinformation campaigns.
- **Collaboration between governments and tech firms** to regulate AI misuse.

The Risk of Emergent, Unpredictable Behavior

One of the **biggest security concerns** in MAS is **emergent behavior**—where agents **act in unexpected ways** when interacting in large numbers.

For example, in 2017, Facebook researchers observed that AI agents **created their own language** that humans couldn't understand. While this was an innocent side effect of optimizing for efficiency, similar unpredictable behaviors could be dangerous if MAS operate in **critical infrastructure, military settings, or financial markets**.

To mitigate this, MAS must be **rigorously tested in simulations** before deployment and continuously monitored in real-world scenarios.

Building Ethical and Secure Multi-Agent Systems

Despite these challenges, researchers are actively developing **ethical and secure frameworks for MAS**. Some best practices include:

- **Regulatory frameworks**: Governments and AI organizations are working on guidelines for **responsible MAS deployment**.
- **Ethical AI research**: Leading AI labs are exploring ways to integrate **human ethics into MAS decision-making**.
- **Security-first AI design**: New AI models are being built with **security measures integrated from the ground up**.

MAS holds **tremendous potential**, but ensuring they are **ethical, secure, and transparent** will be crucial in shaping their future role in society.

10.3 Final Thoughts and Next Steps

Multi-agent systems (MAS) are no longer just an academic curiosity or a futuristic vision. They are transforming industries, from **robotics and transportation to finance and healthcare**. These systems offer **unparalleled coordination, adaptability, and automation**, but they also come with challenges—both technical and ethical.

Throughout this book, we've explored the foundations of MAS, their real-world applications, and the tools needed to build and optimize them. As we wrap up, let's take a step back and reflect on what's next for you as a developer, researcher, or enthusiast in this space.

The Evolution of Multi-Agent Systems

Over the past decade, MAS research has evolved rapidly. Early MAS focused on **rule-based coordination**, but modern systems leverage **machine learning, reinforcement learning, and evolutionary strategies** to improve agent decision-making.

One of the biggest shifts has been the **integration of MAS with deep learning and large-scale distributed computing**. This combination has led to breakthroughs in:

- **Autonomous robots** that work collaboratively in warehouses.
- **Decentralized financial agents** that optimize stock trading strategies.
- **Smart city infrastructure** that manages traffic and energy grids dynamically.

But as MAS continue to evolve, so do the challenges. Security, transparency, and ethical decision-making will be key areas of focus in the coming years.

Bridging Theory and Practice

While understanding the theoretical aspects of MAS is important, real-world implementation is where the real challenge lies. Designing effective multi-agent systems requires **hands-on experience, experimentation, and adaptation**.

If you're new to MAS development, the best way to get started is by **building small-scale simulations** before scaling up. Open-source frameworks like **Mesa, PettingZoo, and Ray RLlib** provide excellent starting points.

For those already working with MAS, consider exploring **hybrid approaches**, where traditional agent-based models are enhanced with **machine learning and game-theoretic strategies**.

Next Steps in Your MAS Journey

Where do you go from here? That depends on your goals:

- **If you want to build MAS-powered applications**, focus on mastering agent frameworks and integrating them with real-world data.
- **If you're interested in research**, explore how MAS can improve areas like swarm intelligence, distributed AI, and cooperative learning.
- **If you're working on AI ethics and security**, think about how MAS can be made fair, transparent, and resilient to adversarial attacks.

MAS is an exciting field because it sits at the intersection of **AI, distributed computing, and real-world decision-making**. Whether you're developing intelligent robots, optimizing supply chains, or designing game-theoretic AI, the future of MAS is in your hands.

This book has given you the tools and knowledge to **begin your journey**. Now, it's up to you to experiment, innovate, and push the boundaries of what multi-agent systems can achieve.